P9-EDP-197

GEMS & MINERALS
OF THE BIBLE

e Lore and Mystery of the Minerals
d Jewels of Scripture, from Adamant to Zircon

uth V. Wright and
obert L. Chadbourne

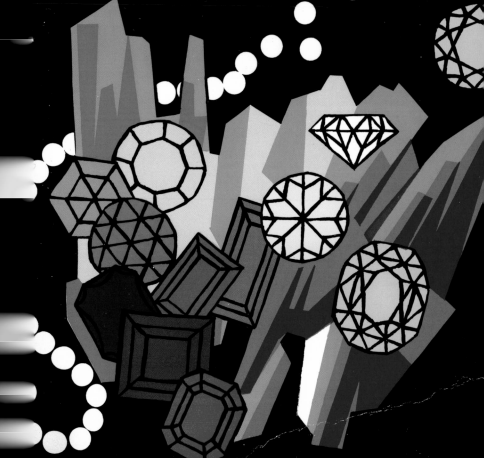

GEMS AND MINERALS OF THE BIBLE

GEMS AND

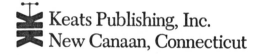
Keats Publishing, Inc.
New Canaan, Connecticut

MINERALS
OF THE BIBLE

RUTH V. WRIGHT
ROBERT L. CHADBOURNE

Quotations from Scripture are from the following versions:

The Amplified Bible. Copyright © 1965 by Zondervan Publishing House. The Amplified Gospel of John copyright © 1954 by The Lockman Foundation; The Amplified New Testament copyright © 1958 by The Lockman Foundation; The Amplified Old Testament Part Two copyright © 1962 by Zondervan Publishing House; The Amplified Old Testament Part One copyright © 1964 by Zondervan Publishing House.

J. B. Phillips, *The New Testament in Modern English.* Copyright © 1958, 1959, 1960, by J. B. Phillips.

The Holy Bible (Douay Version). Translated from the Latin Vulgate. The Old Testament first published by the English College at Douay, 1609. The New Testament first published by the English College at Rheims, 1582. Copyright 1914 by John Murphy Company; reprinted by P. J. Kenedy & Sons.

The Jerusalem Bible. Copyright © 1966 by Darton, Longman & Todd, Ltd. and Doubleday & Company, Inc.

The New English Bible with the Apocrypha. Copyright © The Delegates of the Oxford University Press and The Syndics of the Cambridge University Press, 1961, 1970.

The Holy Bible, Revised Standard Version. Old Testament Section, copyright 1952 by Division of Christian Education of the National Council of the Churches of Christ in the United States of America; New Testament Section, copyright 1946 by the Division of Christian Education of the National Council of the Churches of Christ in the United States of America.

The Complete Bible: An American Translation. Old Testament translated by J. M. Powis Smith and a group of Scholars, The Apocrypha and The New Testament translated by Edgar J. Goodspeed. Copyright 1923, 1927, 1948 by The University of Chicago.

The Bible: A New Translation by James Moffatt. Copyright 1954 by James Moffatt. Published by Harper & Row.

The Holy Bible, Revised Version. Published by John C. Winston Co., 1895.

ACKNOWLEDGMENTS

The original suggestion for *Gems and Minerals of the Bible* came from Mrs. Adeline Bachoroski and Pastor Daryl Schmidt of Rock of Ages Lutheran Church, Colorado Springs. We owe them a debt of immeasurable gratitude, and we hope this book is partial payment of our obligation.

Very special thanks are due to Mr. A. Paul Davis of St. Louis for his generous permission to use the color illustration of the high priest's breastplate from his book *Aaron's Breastplate*. The unmatched replica, valued and insured for $30,000, was presented to the American Baptist Assembly, Green Lake, Wisconsin, where it is exhibited.

To the many co-workers and friends who graciously extended to us the use of their personal libraries and manuscripts and to those who have consistently given their encouragement and assistance, we express our heartfelt appreciation.

Mrs. Mildred Owen deserves our thanks for her skillful editing of the manuscript for the press.

It is difficult to express the extent of our gratitude to Miss Eleanor Jordan, editor. It was her unfailing patience, sound advice, and gentle prodding that brought this work to completion.

R.V.W.
R.L.C.

ABBREVIATIONS

A.B.   *The Amplified Bible*

A.V.   *Authorized (King James) Version*

D.V.   *The Holy Bible: Douay Version*

J.B.   *The Jerusalem Bible*

M.E.   J. B. Phillips, *The New Testament in Modern English*

MOFFATT   James Moffatt, *The Bible: A New Translation*

N.E.B.   *The New English Bible with the Apocrypha*

R.S.V.   *The Holy Bible, Revised Standard Version*

R.V.   *Revised Version*

S.-G.   Smith-Goodspeed, *The Complete Bible: An American Translation*

PREFACE

The King James Version of the Scriptures has an astonishing total of 1,704 references to gemstones and minerals under 124 Greek and Hebrew names. Some of these references are to gems whose names are obscure and whose identity is uncertain, such as adamant or ligure. Others include those of increasing importance—gold, copper, iron, sulfur, and precious gems. Modern versions have used the names of gems more familiar to us, and mention gems and minerals which were known to ancient peoples —jade, turquoise, lapis lazuli, and zircon. We have included several of these more recently used names in our book, for we have studied many Bible versions. The correctness of such modern names has been verified by scientists and archaeologists. Even as our book goes to press, the entire *New English Bible* (including the Old Testament) has just been released, and names of gems are given there for which we have no chapters. Other translations may bring more changes in names.

Throughout the sketchy and often incomplete chapters of the story of man's development from prehistoric days to present times are mentions of minerals or rocks and the uses to which he put them. From the first crudely chipped stone tools to the sophisticated uses of exotic minerals by modern man a long but fascinating tale unfolds. Among the prosaic materials, such as clay and iron, so necessary for man's continued advance in skills, flashes the beauty of gold, silver, and copper, and the color and brilliance of precious and semiprecious gems—turquoise, coral, lapis, and agate, and later, the exquisite beauty of the diamond, emerald, ruby, and sapphire.

The roads by which the valued gems and minerals of the ancients traveled so long ago are fascinating! Beginning in prehistoric times, trade routes were established by the second millennium B.C., by both land and water, across many of the lands of Bible times. Perhaps the first of the ancient gem materials to find its way thousands of miles from its place of origin was amber. Baltic amber traders are believed to have established their routes more than nine thousand years ago. About three thousand years later, Babylonian dealers in lapis lazuli and Egyptian traders bartering turquoise, established trade with other cultures. Even ancient glass was found 2,000 miles from its source of manufacture. Tin was brought by Phoenician sailors from the British Isles to the Mediterranean area. Ancient caravans may have brought gems from India and gold from Africa. Knowledge and cultural developments followed the trade routes.

Many inaccuracies exist as to the sources of ancient gems and minerals. Centers where gems were marketed or cut were frequently regarded as their source, though that may have been far away. Ancient authors related many legends and unusual tales about gems, giving them remarkable medicinal and curative effects as well as telling of superstitions about their ability to protect their owner or wearer from misfortune. Pliny the Elder, whose book *Natural History* is regarded by modern scientists as a mass of misinformation, compiled the writings of even more ancient authors, giving information and beliefs held by people for hundreds of years. His work continued to be regarded as authoritative for another sixteen hundred years. We have found his writings and those of other ancient historians of much interest.

In our research we have discovered amazing and ingenious uses of minerals and gems by very early man. His expert shaping and carving of gems with the crudest of tools seems unbelievable. We have had to smile at his beliefs in their magic. We have learned much of the misconceptions and mistranslations of older Scriptural versions and endeavored to clarify them, delighted when many newer translations bore out our beliefs. We have read early Greek and Roman writers to secure word pictures of their times and to understand their limited scientific knowledge. Yet with all the study and research, we have been unable to fill in many gaps of history and knowledge of Bible times and the minerals and gems known and used then. You, the reader, will realize this, but we hope you will find what we have written interesting, informative, and in a measure, inspiring.

R.V.W.

R.L.C.

CONTENTS

1. ADAMANT

Adamant: a very hard stone or substance of ancient times, possibly corundum.

Yea, they made their hearts as an adamant stone, lest they should hear the law. . . .
Zechariah 7:12, A.V.

Adamant—the mystery mineral! To what mineral family did it belong? Perhaps we will never know. In the mineral sense, it is a term of very doubtful meaning. No evidence exists to identify it specifically with any well-known mineral. Adamant, though not listed in modern mineral texts, was probably a familiar mineral in early Biblical days, for another reference says, "As an adamant harder than flint have I made thy forehead . . ." (Ezek. 3:9, A.V.) A very hard stone is indicated, perhaps corundum. Corundum is second only to the diamond in hardness on Moh's scale of hardness, and includes the sapphire and ruby among its best-known members.

Today, "adamant" means exceedingly hard, unyielding, and hardhearted. Its synonym is "diamond." Although "adamantine luster" is a commonly used mineralogical term to describe the diamond-like luster of minerals, it too is of modern usage. Some authorities assert that adamant was the diamond, but it is highly unlikely that this hardest of gems was known or used in Old Testament times.

The first definite reference to the diamond was recorded by the Latin poet Manilius about A.D. 12. Later, Pliny the Elder (A.D. 23–79) described unmistakably the new bipyramidal (octahedral) crystals from India in his work *Natural History* (about A.D. 77). With no known earlier references to the diamond as we know it, it seems that the diamond was not the adamant (*adamas*) of ancient times and was known only rarely in the time of Pliny.

In apparent contradiction of these facts, housed in the British Museum is a lovely, graceful statue of a girl, dating back to about 480 B.C. Her

1

eyes are two tiny, colorless, uncut precious stones believed to be diamonds. It is likely that her creator was unable to distinguish one colorless, transparent stone from another, and perhaps he chose these for brilliance and similarity.

Speculation has attached a number of minerals to the Biblical adamant. Pliny mentioned another possibility when he referred to *adamas siderites,* since siderite is an iron compound (iron carbonate). In the writings of some of Pliny's predecessors, the term *adamas* is used as the equivalent of iron. Virgil (70–19 B.C.), for example, in describing the doorposts of Avernus, believed to be one of the entrances to the lower world, noted them to be "solid adamant," evidently meaning iron. Later authors seem to have considered adamant to be magnetite or lodestone (magnetic iron ore), for they referred to its magnetic qualities in unmistakable phrases. Shakespeare, in *A Midsummer Night's Dream,* wrote, "You draw me, you hard-hearted adamant."

The Greeks also noted the exceptional hardness of adamant in giving the stone the name *adamantus,* which literally translated means "unconquerable" or "untamable." Later, the Romans gave the name The Invincible to the material. These two nations gave the title "adamant" (invincible) to quite a number of hard minerals, including quartz, emery, hematite, and some transparent gems. Theophrastus (372–287 B.C.), a Greek naturalist who wrote about stones, called *adamas* a carbuncle because of "its not being injured by the Fire."

In the original writings of the Old Testament, adamant was represented by two different Hebrew words: *yăhălōm,* which meant a stone of great value and brilliancy, and *shämîr,* which related to something very hard but had no definite connection with the first word. The latter word recalls the old Hebrew legend in the Talmud of the miraculous instrument the Shämîr, which Aaron used to cut the stones in the high priest's breastplate.

The ancients must have valued engraving tools highly, since they engraved many of their gems, as well as other stones. Jeremiah's reference, "The sin of Judah is written with a pen of iron, and with the point of a diamond . . ." (17:1, A.V.), was probably a figurative expression in which a stylus with a hardened tip of iron was contrasted with one which possessed a tip of some other hard material. The instrument, undoubtedly used for engraving stone, likely had a small chip or flake of corundum as the hard material at its tip, thus enabling the stylus to cut or drill easily into any other material. One can readily understand why the instrument should have earned the ancient Hebrew epithet "the smiter." The Greeks, in translating the Old Testament, gave to this valuable engraving tool the descriptive title "adamantine claw."

See Diamond; Sapphire.

2. AGATE

Agate: a semiprecious stone of the quartz family, highly valued by ancient civilizations.

And thou shalt make the breastplate of judgment with cunning work; . . . And thou shalt set in it settings of stones, even four rows of stones. . . . And the third row a ligure, an agate, and an amethyst. *Exodus 28:15, 17, 19, A.V.*

Are you terrified by the violence of thunderstorms or fearful of the bite of some of the dangerous spiders of the Mediterranean area? Had you lived in one of the early civilizations, you would probably have carried an amulet of agate blessed by a priest. Amulets were closely associated with the religious beliefs of the ancients, who thought that agate had the power to protect one from spiders and storms.

Many a caravan traveler would have advised you to carry an agate pebble in your mouth to suck upon and so allay your thirst as you rode a swaying camel over the waterless wastes. If this method worked, the effect was largely psychological.

As strange as the superstitions that surround it were the explanations given to account for the formation of agate. Some of the ancients thought that red-colored agates were the solidified blood of demons and were capable of warding off evil spirits. Others believed that agates of all colors formed in the bodies of animals. Others explained agate as being numerous natural substances transformed to stone.

Differences of opinion continue to exist concerning the formation of agate. One plausible explanation holds that open ducts in the walls of a cavity in volcanic rock permit silica-laden waters to enter, which on evaporation deposit a thin layer of mineral within the cavity. Repetition of the process results in deposition of layer after layer of multihued quartz until the cavity is completely filled. Cavities (vesicles) occur in great numbers in lava (igneous) rocks. These vesicles, formed by expanding volcanic gases, become ideal spots for the deposition of agate by circulating groundwaters. One argument against this theory maintains that many agates exhibit no apparent channel by which the silica-saturated waters could enter, leave their burden of mineral, and depart.

Thunder eggs, an interesting type of agate, possibly formed as described, exhibit color in irregular patches. Other agate nodules molded by the cavities in which they formed frequently show wavy, concentric bands of varying shades and colors. Agate is a form of chalcedony, the fine-grained variety of quartz.

The Sumerians, the first known inhabitants of Mesopotamia, preceding the Hebrews by many centuries, were the earliest users of agate and other semiprecious quartz gems. They achieved fine cutting and polishing of these stones, making them into beads, cylinder seals, signet rings, and other articles of jewelry. Agate and carnelian beads must have been quite popular, since large numbers have been recovered from archaeological sites. Many beads were cylindrical in shape, often two or more inches in length and beautifully carved. The drilling was accomplished by means of a crude bow drill, yet it was amazingly true and precise.

Other peoples following the Sumerians continued to use quantities of agate. Numerous engraved amulets or talismans, carved seals, signets, and finger rings, many having magical inscriptions or symbolical figures incised upon them, have been found.

Agate is named as the eighth stone in the breastplate of the high priest by most versions of the Bible. However, A. Paul Davis selected a blue sapphire for this breastplate gem.

Other agate items were often of rare beauty. Archaeologists have found goblets, cups, bottles, bowls, and some carved figures created by artisans of these ancient civilizations. In later Roman times, Pliny commented that drug dispensers used agate mortars and pestles to grind herbs and drugs, a practice surviving to the present day.

The first recorded systematic search for agate was made by the Egyptians about 3500 B.C., when it was gathered from the desert areas near Gebel Abn Diyeiba and Aswan. Agate was traded among the Arabians and neighboring peoples around 500 B.C. Probably their principal source was India, where agate of magnificent quality, weathering out of igneous rock, was plentiful and easily collected.

Theophrastus was the first person known to describe agate in writing. He refers to it as a "marvelously beautiful stone," held and sold at high value, and attributed the name as being derived from the Greek name of the River Achates, in Sicily, where as early as 300 B.C. quantities of agate material had been collected. Pliny discussed agate and mentioned numerous localities where it had been discovered. The plentiful supply reduced both its value and popularity.

In the United States fine agate comes from the Lake Superior region. In Oregon, Antelope and the Warm Springs Indian Reservation provide fine cabinet specimens, and the agate beaches are famous. The Mint Canyon and Soledad Canyon area 50 miles north of Los Angeles yields splendid fortification agates. Agates are found in glacial drift in prairie states, and there are localities in Minnesota, Illinois, Wyoming, Idaho, and elsewhere.

3. ALABASTER

Alabaster: compact gypsum of fine texture, usually white and translucent.

Jesus himself was now in Bethany in the house of Simon the leper. As he was sitting at table, a woman approached him with an alabaster flask of very costly spikenard perfume. She broke the neck of the flask and poured the perfume on Jesus' head. Mark 14:3, M.E.

The touching story of the anointing of Jesus with precious, perfumed ointment is told by all four Gospel writers. All except John mention the alabaster box or flask, a common container in those days for ointments, oils, perfumes, and cosmetics. While most English translations of the Bible suggest the actual breaking of the flask at the time of Jesus' anointing, some Biblical students believe only the seal was broken.

Alabaster was a favorite material for the carving of lovely objects, as well as ornamentation in building, over a long period of history in Mediterranean lands. It is surprising that no mention is made of it in the Authorized Version of the Old Testament. However, the Revised Standard Version tells of the use of alabaster for statuary in the exquisite poetry of the Song of Solomon, as the maiden describes her lover: "His arms are rounded gold, set with jewels. His body is ivory work, encrusted with sapphires. His legs are alabaster columns set upon bases of gold" (5:14–15, R.S.V.).

In the ruins of Nineveh, more than 700 palace halls have been re-explored by the Oriental Institute of the University of Chicago. Here, reliefs carved in alabaster, delineating scenes from Assyrian history, extend nearly two miles.

King Tutankhamen's tomb, discovered by Sir Howard Carter in 1922, has yielded many alabaster treasures. One is a portrait head of the king, a stopper to seal a well in a funerary chest. Another magnificent item is a drinking cup of alabaster, carved as a half-open lotus flower, with buds forming the handles. A painted wooden gosling breaking from an egg in an alabaster nest was also discovered. An intimate item relating to King Tutankhamen is an intricately carved, ibex-headed alabaster boat, whose purpose it was to carry the heaven-bound king along the celestial Nile. A nude maiden guarded a canopied miniature sarcophagus and a canopic chest of alabaster holding four miniature coffins which contained the king's preserved organs, except the heart.

The beautiful jars, boxes, vases, and flasks of these ancient peoples were given the name "alabastra." As often happens, time brought a change of usage, and the name "alabastra" was applied to many articles without regard to the material of which they were made.

Alabaster's use from days of antiquity as a durable though easily worked material continues to be illustrated. In 1951, Bernard Bothmer, of the Brooklyn Museum, advised the Virginia Museum of Fine Arts in Richmond to purchase a portion of an alabaster statue. Beautifully carved, the statue (the upper part of the body) was of Sèma-Tawytefnakht of the court of King Psamtik I of Egypt about 2,500 years ago. Mr. Bothmer began searching for the lower half, which had been broken off at the elbows and across the abdomen centuries earlier. In 1952, in Paris, seeing a picture of crossed legs with hands resting on the calves, he realized this was the missing part of the statue. He continued his hunt, finally learning it was privately owned in Luxor, Egypt. For four years he negotiated for the remainder of the figure. On April 2, 1965, the complete statue went on display in Richmond, Virginia. It is a handsome, relaxed figure, hands resting on crossed legs, grinning happily at today's world.

A massive variety of gypsum, resembling marble, alabaster is much softer and more translucent. Beautiful snowy gypsum, a massive gypsum especially free of impurities, is of a very light color with exceedingly small crystals producing a smooth, fine-grained mass. When highly polished, it presents a velvety finish and even texture. Although chiefly used for the carving of art objects, alabaster was also employed as an exceptionally beautiful building material.

Alabaster, formerly known as "alabastrites," was quarried and worked at Alabastron, a locality near Thebes on the upper Nile in Egypt, near King Tutankhamen's tomb.

Some Colorado cities have alabaster deposits literally in their back-yards. In Owl Canyon, near Fort Collins, Colorado, is the largest alabaster quarry in the United States. Alabaster of good quality has been mined here for years to make attractive souvenirs. The best material is turned on lathes to make artistic objets d'art. The finest Colorado alabaster, pink in color, is mottled and veined, so it is a very attractive material for the fashioning of these items.

4. AMBER

Amber: a yellow to orange-brown translucent gem material; ancient name of "electrum" denoted its peculiar electrical qualities; is actually the solidified and fossilized resin of extinct varieties of coniferous trees.

And I looked, and behold, a whirlwind came out of the north, a great cloud, and a fire infolding itself, and a brightness was about it, and out of the midst thereof as the colour of amber, out of the midst of the fire. *Ezekiel 1:4, A.V.*

The words "sea gold" bring to mind pictures of full-rigged ships breast-ing the waves, bloody hand-to-hand battles on heaving decks, and the captured cargoes of treasure-laden galleons sailing home to Spain. Yet sea gold is not the stolen treasure of marauding pirates. It is amber, the ancient gem material scooped up by fishermen from the stormy waters of the Baltic Sea from times long past man's memory to the present day.

Amber is one of the oldest gemstones. Archaeologists have shown that it was used for amulets which have been found in the tombs of Stone Age men. Of rich color, its peculiar electrical qualities made it magical to primitive man, who longed to possess it. Widespread trade in amber developed as early as 9,000 years ago when Scandinavian sailors and amber traders of the Baltic area carried it along the important river routes to the Mediterranean, reaching Knossos, Crete, the world's marketplace of those days. Then hardy Phoenician traders bartered for it, bearing it to every profitable port on the inland sea. Baltic amber found in Cretan archaeological sites illustrates the lengthy journeys made by the highly prized material.

The famous city of Mycenae, Greece, yielded much amber when its ruins were excavated. Writings from those days in Mediterranean lands indicate that amber beads were considered a cure for goiter. Surprisingly, they are still occasionally purchased for this reason. Amber was highly prized as a pendant, more for its protection against witchcraft than for its glowing beauty.

Pliny argued, correctly, that amber was the resin of pine trees, but he thought the trees were still living. He was skeptical of ancient beliefs about amber's origin: the tears of a particular bird, solidified urine of the lynx, coagulated sea-foam, the slime of some unknown, mysterious lake. He was positive about its potent medicinal uses. Salve of amber and Attic honey improved dim sight, and amber pulverized and drunk in water cured diseases of the stomach. Pliny also described amber's peculiar magnetic attraction. Amber, when rubbed rapidly between the fingers, draws to itself straw and dry leaves.

Amber may have had ritualistic uses in ancient times because of its flammability, replacing pine wood shavings used by the Greeks and Romans in kindling the holy hearthfire. It was burned as incense, and women of early civilizations often carried lumps of amber, rubbing them to induce its distinctive fragrance.

Amber is a fossil resin from prehistoric pine trees, formed in the Tertiary and later geological periods. Pine forests covered Northern Europe, and in some areas are still extensive. These trees, like their modern relatives, exuded great amounts of resin. As the resin oozed through the bark of the trees, it formed irregular lumps, creating a fascinating and accurate history book! Inquisitive insects, entrapped in the sticky, golden-colored gum, were completely encased as the resin continued to flow. When the resin had changed to amber, their bodies became perfectly preserved in the most minute detail.

Amber containing an insect was among the most valued possessions of ancient peoples, who believed it warded away witchcraft. Modern people doubt the magic but nevertheless place great value on amber with inclusions. The museum at the University of Könisberg in East Prussia had more than 70,000 fine specimens. This remarkable exhibit was unfortunately destroyed during World War II. Many insects found in those ancient forests, or related species, still exist today: ants, mosquitoes, flies, and roaches have been found; spiders (small arachnids) have been preserved in amber and are much like their modern descendants. Even a famous fossil flea, the only one known to science, was found entrapped in its amber tomb. Seeds, pine needles, bits of wood, and flowerlets have been found embedded in the amber, giving much information about those very ancient times.

The altered resin known as amber is found in a sedimentary deposit called "blue earth" which underlies the region southeast of the Baltic Sea and outcrops under the shallow offshore area of that body.

While the Authorized Version describes the brightness of the fiery whirlwind "as the colour of amber" other versions describe the color as that of shining or glowing metal or gleaming bronze. The ancient name "electrum" meant the alloy of gold and silver as well as amber. Certainly a beautiful golden glow is meant in Ezekiel.

5. AMETHYST

Amethyst: a clear lavender to bluish violet variety of crystal quartz with many degrees of color intensity, when deeply colored, one of the most attractive of gems.

The foundations of the wall of the city were garnished with all manner of precious stones . . . the twelfth, an amethyst. Revelation 21:19, 20, A.V.

The Deceiver was a name given to amethyst in the early ages of history. Its reputation was gained by a most unusual use given to the gem. On festive occasions, when noblemen had imbibed too much, water—or at least cheap watered-down wine—was sometimes substituted for wine in amethyst goblets. The glowing purple of the amethyst created the illusion of good wine. Since the serving of water in amethyst goblets was generally known, it may account for the words of the steward at the wedding at Cana, who exclaimed, late in the feast when serving the wine created by Jesus' first miracle, ". . . 'Every man serves the good wine first; and when men have drunk freely, then the poor wine; but you have kept the good wine until now'" (John 2:10, R.S.V.).

Ancient artists accomplished a seemingly impossible task in carving with simple tools beautiful goblets from amethyst crystals, some of exceptional size and engraved with elaborate designs. Amethyst was also carved into exquisite vases, charms, intaglios, and miniatures by the Egyptians and Romans, and the Babylonians frequently carried amulets of amethyst.

Although the various translations of the Bible disagree on the names of several Biblical gems, every Bible version agrees on the name "amethyst," and it continues in use today. Not only has the stone's Biblical use been described in its adornment of the foundation walls of the New Jerusalem, but it is also one of the stones (the ninth) used in decorating the high priest's breastplate.

Widely held beliefs in early days attributed magical properties to the gem. The Hebrews, whose name for amethyst was *'ăhlämäh*, "dream," believed it induced pleasant dreams, and the Greeks considered it an antidote for drunkenness. Pliny suggested that the Greek name *ame-thustos*, "not drunken," was given to the stone because the color was similar to, though not attaining, the hue of wine.

Amethyst was scarce and greatly prized in ancient civilizations. The most likely source of supply for the inhabitants of Israel was the island of Ceylon, the treasure house of gems. Pliny believed the finest amethysts came from India and a part of Arabia adjoining Syria. In modern times, extensive deposits of good-quality material have been found in Brazil, causing the gem to become relatively plentiful and consequently cheaper in price.

Catherine the Great of Russia, famed for her amethysts, secured her magnificent collection from mines in the Ural Mountains. England's Queen Charlotte wore a lovely necklace of amethyst beads, a historical piece of jewelry, valued in the eighteenth century at $10,000, though perhaps of much less value today. The large amethyst which adorns the crown of England known as St. Edward's crown is the oldest of the crown jewels and goes back to at least 1042, when it was worn by Edward the Confessor.

Amethyst's glowing color made it highly valued for thousands of years, and it was especially popular in Greek and Roman times. It has been a traditional stone in rings of religious leaders. To anyone familiar with the lovely gem, the wide variation of shading is truly amazing, for it ranges from amethystine, with a barely perceptible tinting, to a most intense purple. The deep purple varieties are without peer in nature, making it one of the most valuable of the quartz gems.

Amethyst's color was once thought to be due to the presence of traces of manganese, but exhaustive tests failed to detect this element. Today some authorities believe the internal structure accounts for the color, the crystal being made up of minutely thin layers which alternately bend the penetrating light rays first in one direction and then the opposite. Most experts, however, incline to the radioactivity theory in accounting for the purple hue. Experiments with these emanations produce some amazing and unexplainable changes in quartz. Sometimes clear quartz crystals, bombarded with radioactive rays, turn to amethyst color, and at other times to a smoky hue. Another behavior of this mineral is an intriguing puzzle. Why, when heated, will one amethyst crystal turn a golden color while another becomes light green?

As with other quartz minerals, there are numerous occurrences of amethyst in the United States. Several states have fairly extensive deposits, such as Amherst County, Virginia; Alexander and Lincoln counties in North Carolina; Yellowstone National Park; the Keweenaw Peninsula of Michigan; Jefferson County, Montana; and Oxford County, Maine. Deposits of fine amethyst are found in Uruguay, where it is the national gem, and in Brazil, making this lovely gem available to all.

6. ANTIMONY

Antimony: a bright, silvery-white, metallic element; Biblical mention of it probably refers to stibnite, the mineral composed of antimony and sulfur.

O afflicted one, storm-tossed, and not comforted, behold, I will set your stones in antimony, and lay your foundations with sapphires. Isaiah 54:11, R.S.V.

Several brightly colored paintings adorned the walls of the old Egyptian tomb, depicting the career of the person buried there. Hieroglyphic inscriptions identified the occupant as Khnum Hotep, ruler of a district of Egypt under Sesostris II about 1900 B.C. Most of the paintings on the plastered walls depicted the nobleman hunting, dancing, and harvesting. One was startlingly unlike the others. It showed two Egyptian officials introducing a group of foreigners to the ruler. Much different in looks from their hosts, the visitors had thick black hair, pointed beards, and sharper features and were clothed in unfamiliar costumes.

A hieroglyphic inscription explains the scene. Thirty-seven Asiatics have arrived, bringing a very special gift to the Egyptian ruler. The leader of the group, Ibsha, sheik of the highlands, bears a Semitic name and the other members of his caravan are obviously Semites. They have traveled with their animals to the Egyptian court, perhaps to procure trade, and bearing a rare and valued gift of eyepaint now known as kohl. This is one of the earliest recorded allusions to the antimony mineral, stibnite (stibium), so widely used as an eye cosmetic.

In 1890, Percy A. Newberry, a British archaeological expert, discovered a large rock chamber, used as a tomb, after lengthy digging to excavate ancient burial sites at Beni Hasan on the banks of the Nile River, 168 miles south of Cairo.

Only one English version of the Holy Scriptures, the Revised Standard, mentions the mineral antimony: ". . . I will set your stones in antimony, and lay your foundations with sapphires" (Isa. 54:11). The Authorized Version translates the phrase as: "I will lay thy stones with fair colours." Bible students suggest that the use of "antimony" in the Revised Standard Version in this instance is probably used poetically as Isaiah searches for adequate words in foretelling the beauty and splendor of the New Jerusalem. The term is used to take the place of mortar which would set off the great beauty of the stones composing the wall of the city.

The Revised Standard Version and other English translations fail to use the term "antimony" in three instances where one might expect to find the mineral mentioned. The Douay and Spanish Language versions, however, specifically mention it in the two similar passages which refer to Jezebel, describing her as painting her eyes or painting her face (II Kings 9:30; Jer. 4:30). The Douay Version gives the term as "stibic-stone" (stibnite).

Antimony was widely used by ancient peoples in numerous ways. It was a well-known mineral thousands of years before the birth of Christ, and its use is attested to by its appearance in a Chaldean vase dated approximately 4000 B.C., illustrating that metalworkers of those long-ago days knew how to secure the metal from its ores. In ancient Egypt, vessels of antimony were used to carry water from the wells, while Egyptian women, of course, made a cosmetic from the mineral.

Antimony was an important constituent of much of the glass manufactured during days of antiquity. Many glassmakers in the early periods of glassmaking were itinerant, and glass made with similar materials is found in widely separated areas. A magnificent glass diatretum (cage cup) was carved to show the 400-foot-high mariner's beacon of Alexandria, Egypt, with the towering statue of Poseidon atop it, the original lighthouse being one of the Seven Wonders of the World. But the beautiful cup was excavated in Afghanistan, at Begram, 2,400 miles east of Egypt. The design indicated that the large cup may have been made near Alexandria, reaching Begram as a gift or art piece. A tiny sliver of the glass, carefully analyzed, revealed it was a high-antimony type of glass, unknown in Afghanistan but very familiar to the Roman world.

Antimony was used from the second millennium B.C. to achieve opacity in glass of many colors. Later, during the sixth century B.C., antimony was discovered to make glass colorless when a rise in temperature was produced. For several centuries it was widely used in Roman lands for this purpose.

Antimony is usually found in nature in the form of stibnite, an attractive mineral of lead-gray color which forms interesting crystals, the finest coming from Japan.

Antimony is commonly used today in linotype machines; it is mixed with lead to form cast newspaper type because it increases the hardness and strength of the lead and has a low melting point. Such lead-antimony (type metal) alloys have the additional desirable property of expansion on cooling. This ensures that the molded type will be remarkably sharp. Widely used in our modern economy, it is alloyed with lead for storage battery plates and is used as a pigment in paint, enamels, and glass. Antimony is an agent in flameproofing textiles and in some methods of rubber vulcanizing. Its compounds appear in matches, percussion caps, and fireworks. But antimony's most unusual use is as a component of camouflage paints, where it has the peculiar property of reflecting infrared rays exactly as green vegetation does.

See Stibic-Stone.

7. ASPHALT

Asphalt: an organic material in the form of mineral pitch· blackish-brown or black in color; sticky; varies in consistency from heavy, syrupy liquid to solid material; flows readily when heated; today, usually artificially produced from the distillation of petroleum.

Then, as they had bricks .for stone and asphalt for mortar, they said, "Come on, let us make a name for ourselves by building a city and a tower whose top reaches to heaven." Genesis 11:3–4, Moffatt.

Artificial stone—cement—which blends well with the building material used, is the mortar used today. But sticky black asphalt was the mortar of ancient builders. The material was used by prehistoric people for holding together objects, including building bricks or stones. During the pre-Babylonian cultures of the Euphrates River Valley, 3800–2500 B.C., asphalt was applied to ornaments carved of wood as an adhesive to hold gold foil to them. Mosaics were inlaid in an asphalt backing, and statues were covered with mother-of-pearl and ivory embedded in it.

Asphalt's use on the practical side was as important as its use for creating art treasures. Floors made of a layer of asphalt and clay brick cemented together with asphalt have been found by archaeologists, and asphalt was used as a cementing agent in the wall of Babylon as well as mortar for the Tower of Babel. King Nebuchadnezzar, following the customs of his time in trying to outdo the building feats of his predecessors, constructed a bridge 370 feet long across the Euphrates River. The piers supporting the bridge were built of bricks set in bitumen (asphalt), protected at their bases with asphalt as a waterproofing agent.

Boat and ship builders have used asphalt for centuries for calking their vessels to ensure that they are leakproof and seaworthy. The Lord instructed Noah to calk his ark in such a manner. The ancient bitumen wells at Hit (Iraq) on the Euphrates River are still producing and continue to furnish a kind of asphalt which is used by modern builders of small, round basket-like boats as well as by the ancient builders of many centuries before. These wells, mentioned by the ancient Greek writer Herodotus, are situated about 150 miles above the site of early Babylon.

Through the centuries, as explorers ventured farther and farther from their home ports, asphalt continued to be used for calking and waterproofing their ships. When Christopher Columbus discovered the New World, he found a huge and unusual source of asphalt, which is also called pitch. On his third voyage he stopped at an island in the present West Indies, which he named La Trinidad, where he "careened his galleons and caulked their storm-racked seams with natural waterproofing material." The famous Pitch Lake of Trinidad provided calking material in 1498 and continues to do so. In 1595, Sir Walter Raleigh also located the famous island which pours asphalt into the sea and marveled at the extent of the sealing material. The Spaniards called the port where he landed Tierra de Brea, the Land of Tar. Sir Walter observed that the pitch was of excellent quality, did not melt in the hot sun as did the Norwegian calking substance, and would prove of value in the future. Since his rediscovery of the lake, more than 10 million tons of asphalt have been taken from Pitch Lake. The supply continues to be almost as great, though the level of the lake has dropped about 20 feet in the last century. The strange lake moves constantly—with the motion beginning in the fresh, soft center, called the Mother of the Lake—and is at least 285 feet deep.

After exposure, the soft asphalt hardens to a variety which no longer flows. The hardened material was probably used by Raleigh. Geologists say Pitch Lake has existed for thousands of years. Like other deposits of natural asphalt, Trinidad's lake of asphalt was produced from the mother substance petroleum through a process of evaporation. Scientists produce artificial asphalt through the distillation of petroleum on the same general principle. Though asphalt, bitumen, pitch, and tar, and the archaic slime, differ chemically, perhaps, since they are of very complex composition and vary from one location to another, in general usage the words are employed interchangeably.

Asphalt was used in Biblical lands; its earliest use, however, may have been the third millennium B.C. in India. Sir Mortimer Wheeler, working at a reservoir at Mohenjo-Daro, found that asphalt was used as a water stop between its brick walls. The material was called "earth butter" in early Buddhist traditions. Even in ancient days it was used for flood control. Roads many centuries old used asphalt for surfacing One king left a comment that he had found his kingdom a land of mud, but left it "laced with roads glistening with asphalt."

Lakes of asphalt have served as an excellent preservative also. Bones of prehistoric animals have been found in Pitch Lake. In the United States, at the famous Rancho La Brea, Hancock Park, Los Angeles, California, large numbers of fossils of prehistoric animals have been taken from the tar pits. Deluded into believing the surface secure, hundreds of saber-toothed cats, giant sloths, cave bears, mastodons, woolly mammoths, and elephants were trapped as the light crust broke under their weight and they fell into the sticky tar. Vultures, other birds, tree trunks, and even acorns have also been found.

See Bitumin; Pitch; Slime.

8. BDELLIUM

Bdellium: an unknown substance, probably mineral, which could be any one of a number of minerals; while absolute identification is impossible, it is believed to have been opal.

And the gold of that land is good; their bdellium and the onyx stone. . . . Genesis 2:12, A.V.

If you like guessing games, here is one: Try to pick the correct substance actually represented by the ancient name "bdellium"! Some authorities say it was the pearl; others, an aromatic gum; while modern sources are inclined to believe it meant opal. Since pearl is mentioned many times in the Scriptures, the identification of bdellium as opal appears reasonable, as opal was recognized and used by early cultures.

As early as 500 B.C., Onomacritus mentioned opal in his writings, and Pliny considered the opal next to the emerald in value. His glowing descriptions of it have often been quoted. Though opal was highly esteemed for many centuries and used as a charm against the magic of the "evil eye," eventually wild legends and superstitions destroyed its popularity. The belief that opal could bring ill luck to its possessor began, perhaps, in the sixteenth century. A plague raged in Venice, and opals worn by the victims seemed to brighten just before their deaths. Since heat affects the opal, fever may have caused the gem to glow with unusual brightness, but superstition blamed the stone for the illness.

Sir Walter Scott is credited with having destroyed much of the opal's popularity by using it as a gem of sinister omen worn by Lady Hermione, a character in *Anne of Geierstein*. Following the publication of this novel in 1820, the value of the opal decreased as much as 50 percent. Queen Victoria did much to reestablish its popularity by giving the gem to her daughters as wedding gifts and wearing opals herself in public. With unfounded superstitions largely discredited, opals are regaining their place as beautiful and popular gemstones.

Mexico is the source of lovely fire opals, but in modern times Australia has produced most of the precious opal, exporting about seven million dollars' worth of the gemstone to the United States, Germany, and Japan in 1968. Extensive mining is carried on at several widely separated locations, the most famous being Lightning Ridge, about 365 miles northwest of Sydney, where the famous and beautiful black opals are found.

Recently a major Mexican discovery of a new type of black opal occurring in basalt and resembling peacock feathers in its play of color has given the world a vast supply of material not only for gemstones but also for fairly large carvings. The immense find is a wide fissure in a cliff wall, completely filled with black basalt which is extensively permeated with precious black opal. Extending back into the cliff at least 150 feet, the exposed material extends up the cliff face about 162 feet in a crevice approximately 9 feet wide. The mine has been named, aptly, *Luz Nueva* (New Light).

Many legends regarding opal are unbelievably fantastic, although others have a solid geological foundation. One insists that only in the dry earth bed of an inland sea are opals found, as if the disappearing sea had left this vivid gem in memory of the rainbows often arched above it. Though poetically phrased, this is essentially true. Superstition said that the opal would make the owner invisible, saving him from the dangers of battle.

Opal is a hydrous variety of silica; unlike most precious gem minerals, it occurs in both noncrystalline (amorphous) and partially crystalline forms. It is commonly found in irregular, compact masses in cavities and veins. The body color exhibits quite a range, but a given stone usually has a single color. However, so many hues well up from the depths of precious opal that we speak of them as "colors at play." The shifting change of colors is due to the interference with light rays.

We have been describing precious opal, but we know that opal occurs as a replacement of organic wood fibers, in the same manner as jasper and agate, in the petrification of wood. While this material lacks the play of color so much admired in precious opal, it is of great beauty. Since Asia Minor has produced much wood opal, it is possible that the people of the Bible lands called wood opal "bdellium" and used it widely. Opalite, a material similar to wood opal, is found in several Western states, but precious opal is found in the United States only in Virgin Valley, Nevada. However, any identification of the Biblical "bdellium" is somewhat uncertain, at best.

9 . BERYL

Beryl: a silicate of beryllium and aluminum; occurs in hexagonal, prismatic crystals of great hardness, 7.5 to 8 on the scale of hardness in minerals.

And in the fourth row a beryl, and an onyx, and a jasper: they shall be set in gold in their inclosings. Exodus 28:20, A.V.

Would you like to be amiable, relaxed, and fearless and have your intellect quickened? Do you crave to be victorious in the courts of law and the sports arena or to be protected on the field of battle? Do you wish to invoke the aid of mighty heroes or of the cunning water spirits? If so, you should wear the gem called beryl, for the Egyptians believed it had the power to assure all this and more.

The Hebrews of early Biblical times used beryl as two of the twelve stones in the high priest's breastplate. One was the emerald, a rare and exquisite member of the beryl family, while the other beryl was probably the more common variety aquamarine.

In the description of the foundation stones of the Holy City (Rev. 21), beryl is listed as the eighth stone. Once again we have difficulty in exactly identifying Bible gemstones. The Greek manuscripts and Authorized Version identify beryl with the Hebrew word tărshîsh, while the Vulgate translates tărshîsh as chrysolite (olivine).

We assume it was actually beryl and believe that the Scriptural beryl may have been aquamarine, the most plentiful variety of gem beryl. This gem was highly valued in past civilizations, not alone for its beauty but because of the magical qualities it was supposed to possess. Pliny described the aquamarine as most esteemed because its color was sea green, the color of a calm sea. He also listed the several other hues of beryl. Pliny was the first to surmise that the beryl (aquamarine) and emerald were varieties of the same mineral. While emerald is merely a chromium-bearing beryl, it has such a distinctive color that it seems almost in a class by itself. (See Emerald.)

The aquamarine displays such attractive color qualities that historians have likened it to a thousand leagues of sunlit sea imprisoned in a cup. Since color was the only determining factor among many of the gemstones, numerous gems of similar hues were arbitrarily put in the same classification. It is possible that "beryl" might have denoted blue to bluish-green turquoise. Martin Luther had this opinion!

Beryl crystals usually occur as hexagonal (six-sided) prisms, with the usual termination being flat like a tabletop. Beryl is a silicate of aluminum and beryllium (a chemical element named for the stone). The addition of small traces of other elements produces the glorious individual colors. The blue and light green colors of aquamarine result from the presence of traces of iron. Some of the other distinctively colored varieties of beryl, such as pink and gold, are often considered more desirable than the pale-green or blue variety.

The Bible-mentioned beryl was supposed to have come from Tartesus, Spain, a questionable source. Pliny speaks of other localities: Egypt, India, Ceylon, Kashmir, and Upper Burma. If the famous mines of Egypt near the Red Sea which furnished many magnificent emeralds did not also produce other beryl gems, there must have been other Egyptian sources of beryl. At Dakka on the Nile, beryl beads have been found in predynastic graves.

The Latin word for beryl, *beryllus*, has an Indian origin, probably of Sanskrit derivation. Peculiarly, in medieval Latin, the term *berrilus* was applied not only to beryl but likewise to crystal, spectacles, or an eyeglass.

In 1955 gem hobbyists, Mr. and Mrs. A. Paul Davis and Mr. O. D. Evans, of St. Louis, Missouri, began an intensive study of the Biblical breastplate of the high priest. Drawing from the extensive collection of Mr. Evans, they assembled large and beautiful gems to make a replica of this inspired vestment of Aaron, the first head of the Hebrew priesthood, as described in Exodus 28. Their choice for the beryl mentioned there was a golden beryl.

The completed, beautiful, authentically structured replica of the ancient breastplate is now on permanent exhibit at the American Baptist Foundation at Green Lake, Wisconsin, where a value of more than $30,000 has been placed on it.

In the United States there are numerous localities for beryl, principally in New England. The only true gem aquamarine area is on 14,000-foot Mount Antero, in the Colorado Rockies, southwest of Buena Vista. It is a hardy soul who will brave the rugged slopes, sudden icy storms, sweeping winds, and bitter temperatures to hunt the elusive crystals that are found only above 13,000 feet near the summit of this temperamental mountain.

See Turquoise.

10. BITUMEN

Bitumen: originally a name for mineral pitch or asphalt; now applied to several mineral substances that are inflammable, such as tar and naphtha.

And they said to one another, "Come, let us make bricks, and burn them thoroughly." And they had brick for stone, and bitumen for mortar. Genesis 11:3, R.S.V.

The bricks of the Tower of Babel were joined together with it. The ark built by Noah was waterproofed with it. The infant Moses floated in a basket sealed with it. The fiery furnace that was intended to incinerate Shadrach, Meshach, and Abednego was fired by it (along with other materials). The Egyptians used it in their embalming processes. In the early ages, it was not unusual for neighboring nations to wage war against each other for possession of lands where it was plentiful.

Bitumen is a somewhat archaic term for asphaltum, actually the best waterproofing agent known to man, and it has the additional desirable qualities of being acid-resistant and serving well as an adhesive. In Biblical writings it is also referred to as pitch or slime. Perhaps there is a slight difference between these two, for some was found floating on the surface of the Dead Sea or in the nearby marshes, while other occurrences of the mineral pitch were abundant in some of the dry wadies (valleys) leading to this sea. Curiously, ancient writing often named the present Dead Sea as Lake Asphaltides.

Bitumen, well known to the cultures of olden times, was widely used. It was the cementing agent between the joints of stone blocks used in fortifications, ramparts, and the walls of larger buildings. Bitumen also furnished protection, in the form of waterproofing, to unburned bricks, making them durable and weather-resistant. Workmen who labored to build the Tower of Babel used bitumen to cement the bricks together. *The Jerusalem Bible* presents the story interestingly: "Throughout the earth men spoke the same language, with the same vocabulary. Now as they moved eastwards they found a plain in the land of Shinar where they settled. They said to one another, 'Come, let us make bricks and bake them in the fire'.—For stone they used bricks, and for mortar they used bitumen.—'Come,' they said, 'let us build ourselves a town and a tower with its top reaching heaven. Let us make a name for ourselves, so that we may not be scattered about the whole earth'" (Gen. 11:1-4).

According to Herodotus (484-425 B.C.), the city of Babylon was entirely encompassed by a moat and a double wall. The earth excavated from the moat was made into bricks, fired, and used in constructing the walls. A mat of interwoven reeds was placed on every thirtieth course of bricks. The heated bitumen, used as a cement between the brick courses, was brought into Babylon from the Is, a small tributary of the Euphrates River. At Ashur, the ancient capital of Assyria, 60 miles south of the site of ancient Nineveh, are wells similar to those on the Is.

Both the Egyptians and the Sumerians were superlative artists and created extremely lifelike statues of the human figure. Great care was taken to give a natural facial expression, though some of the materials used may seem unusual. Both peoples made artificial eyes. In some Sumerian heads, the eye sockets were hollowed out and filled with a capsule of bitumen. Seashell was used to make the white of the eyes, and bitumen or lapis lazuli formed the pupils. These materials were embedded in the bitumen capsules, with the bitumen supposed to create the effect of eyelashes. The result was somewhat strange-looking eyes!

Prosaic as the material bitumen is, it was highly prized by nations of old. Of the many extravagant gifts presented to Cleopatra, the land which supplied asphalt, given to her by Marc Anthony, was significantly described as a "gift fit for a queen."

Today's definition of bitumen, while including its occurrence as a natural asphalt, says that it is any one of a number of substances which are obtained as the asphaltic residues in the distillation of coal tar, petroleum, etc. The man-made variety of asphalts, composed of bitumens, are superior for many of today's industrial uses and are widely used by the roofing industry to achieve the most uniform quality for their asphalt shingles and roofing paper. Being moistureproof, bitumen is used to make wrapping paper which ensures that the contents will remain dry. It is also used in the making of floor tiles and blocks and in some paints.

See Asphalt; Pitch; Slime.

11. BRASS

Brass: an alloy consisting of copper and zinc in varying proportions; in the Biblical narratives usually meant bronze.

For the Lord thy God bringeth thee into a good land, . . . a land whose stones are iron, and out of whose hills thou mayest dig brass. *Deuteronomy 8:7, 9, A.V.*

Brass evokes a vivid mental picture of Daniel's three companions being thrown into the fiery furnace, a furnace which might have been the hollowed inside of a monstrous, gleaming, brass idol, casting shimmering heat waves from the roaring flames within, the flames perhaps stimulated by the addition of bitumen from far up the Euphrates River. Or the picture might be the orgy of sacrifice at the fiery maw of a great brazen image to attempt to appease the insatiable appetite of Moloch. Here the children of Ammon sacrificed their first-born sons and daughters to the patron god of the Phoenicians.

To believe the images were brass, however, is far from the truth. This mineral alloy was unknown in early Hebrew times, and it is equally certain that true brass was never used in the construction of the Tabernacle or the Temple. The Biblical term "brass" in every instance refers either to copper or to bronze.

Pliny the Elder describes the making of true brass, but this early description was in the first century after Christ, though the process might have been known earlier. The alloy was introduced just prior to the beginning of the Christian era. A coin of brass dated 20 B.C. is one of the earliest examples of Roman brass. Roman craftsmen made brass by heating a mixture of pulverized zinc ores (which ore the Romans used is unknown to us), charcoal, and granules of copper, carefully keeping the temperature below the melting point of the copper. After the zinc vapor converted the copper to brass, the crucible temperature was raised, and the brass melted. A new alloy of incomparable worth was now available for man's use!

Old civilizations knew comparatively few pure metals, and no close distinction was made among them. Consequently, ancient alloys were prepared not by the fusing of pure metals but by the direct heating and combining of various ores. In the older Hebrew, the word *n^ehōshĕth* signified either copper or the tin-copper alloy bronze. It is not strange that early translators of the Bible used the word "brass" with these two different meanings in mind. This is illustrated in the King James and Revised versions, but later translators are careful to render the term "brass" as copper or bronze.

When Moses described the Promised Land as "a land whose stones are iron and out of whose hills thou mayest dig brass" (Deut. 8:9), the allusion was undoubtedly to copper. Yet it is well known that, with the exception of a small area in the neighborhood of Aleppo, no copper is found in Palestine proper. Moses must have envisioned a much larger territory that the Israelites were to take over, for King Solomon's copper mines, near the Gulf of Aqaba, were at a considerable distance from the heart of the Holy Land.

The widespread adoption of bronze by the Hebrews demanded new and prolific sources of copper. Archaeological surveys were made by Dr. Nelson Glueck in Transjordan and the Negev that revealed interesting information regarding ancient copper localities. In Edom, east and south of the Dead Sea, he discovered copper slag piles and ruins of very old smelting furnaces at several places. He found a huge mass of copper-bearing sandstone at Wadi el-Jariyeh and extensive copper mines at Meneiyeh, Umm el-Amad, and Khirbet Nahas. Prospecting at three localities turned up good ore of mixed malachite and cuprite. Nearby smelting furnaces gave special emphasis to the reference in Job 28:2 (R.S.V.), that says "copper is smelted from the ore."

Ancient Edom lacked suitable fuel, so furnaces were probably fired with huge amounts of dried shrubs. In the area of the Araba (along the Great Rift) immense quantities of copper were mined and smelted during the early Iron Age. There is evidence that the Edomites and Kenites worked these copper ore deposits long before the coming of the Israelites. Such archaeological evidence supports the contention that this was "a land whose stones are iron, and out of whose hills thou mayest dig brass [copper]."

The famous mines of Laurium, Greece, operating as early as 1000 B.C., produced great quantities of a lead ore, galena. With a high silver content, the ore also contained minerals of the zinc, iron, and manganese groups. Though there is no recorded use, it is possible that the occasional addition of zinc ores to the customary bronze minerals resulted in a product approaching brass. This may have been the "fine copper, precious as gold" mentioned in the Book of Ezra. But it never evolved into a specific process, perhaps because zinc, necessary in true brass, was not known in Biblical times as a separate and distinct metal.

See Bronze; Copper.

12. BRIMSTONE

Brimstone (sulfur): a bright yellow nonmetallic element; combines readily with other elements; occurs naturally as crystals, masses, crusts, or powder; burns easily with the suffocating odor of sulfur dioxide.

But the same day that Lot went out of Sodom it rained fire and brimstone from heaven, and destroyed them all. Luke 17:29, A.V.

The roar of destruction was heard 3,000 miles away. Barometers in New York oscillated from the blast 12,000 miles distant. At least 36,000 people died as a cubic mile of rock hurtled 17 miles into the air and waves 50 to 100 feet high rushed from the scene of chaos at 360 miles an hour to crash on adjacent shores. A volcanic-dust cloud circled the earth eight times, causing sunsets of eerie, unearthly beauty on all continents. Ships passing many miles away told of heavy clouds, nearly continuous lightning, and the heavy, nauseous odor of brimstone. Some captains complained that every inch of brasswork on their vessels was blackened and corroded by gases as they passed through the area. Thus the volcanic island Krakatoa destroyed itself on August 27, 1883, in one of the greatest explosions of all times.

"It rained fire and brimstone from heaven and destroyed them all." One shudders at the awfulness of the skies opening and sending horror and destruction upon everything below. It is a vivid reminder of the ruin of cities, from Sodom and Gomorrah, Pompeii and Herculaneum, to modern cities, when fire rained from above, tossed skyward by the tremendous forces unleashed in volcanic activity. In 1902, Mount Pelée, on the island of Martinique, erupted, and more than 30,000 people lost their lives in a few hours. What an outpouring of anger by nature's usually calm forces, interpreted by the ancients as the vengeance of their gods!

"Brimstone" is a term of considerable antiquity used to denote the noxious element sulfur, a mineral more widely used in the service of man than almost any other. The word "brimstone" derives from the Hebrew in a somewhat roundabout manner, coming from the Hebrew gŏphrîth (from gäphǎr), to cover. Biblically, gŏphrîth is properly translated as sulfur (brimstone). Ancient alchemists with their air of mystery used the word "sulfur" to signify the quality of combustibility. Today, brimstone is known as a synonym for sulfur.

Sulfur is often formed as the result of volcanic activity. It occurs in gases pouring out of vents or fumaroles and is deposited as the gases cool. Sulfur can be produced naturally in many other ways, such as in mine fires where on-the-spot roasting of iron pyrite occurs.

The mineral may also be formed by decomposition of the hydrogen sulfide that frequently is carried by hot-water springs. The action of acid-bearing water from volcanic sources on underground sulfur-bearing metallic compounds often creates hydrogen sulfide. It is also formed by the decomposition of sulfate, particularly gypsum (calcium sulfate). This last action is aided by microscopic organisms, since the living processes of the so-called sulfur bacteria result in a separation of sulfur from the sulfates. Consequently, the greatest repositories of sulfur are beds of gypsum and associated limestone rocks, or the regions of active, dormant, or extinct volcanism.

Sulfur is also frequently found in conjunction with bituminous deposits and is present in the gypsum caps of salt domes. In upper Egypt there are deposits of considerable size.

Almost all Biblical accounts use the flammability of sulfur to depict intense destruction, damage, and torment. "The Lord rained upon Sodom and upon Gomorrah brimstone and fire from the Lord out of heaven" (Gen. 19:24, A.V.). The exact location of these two infamous cities is not definitely known, though they were cities of the Jordan Plain. It is believed they were located near the southeast corner of the Dead Sea and were situated in a well-watered garden area. William Albright, noted archaelogist, believes the destruction of the ancient oasis cities occurred in the early Bronze Age at the time of the catastrophe described in Genesis 19. The ruins were probably overwhelmed by the neighboring waters of the Dead Sea. Ezekiel prophesied a similar happening, a punishment in which there would be: "A great shaking in the land of Israel, . . . an overflowing rain, and great hailstones, fire and brimstone" (38:19–22, A.V.). Since in almost every reference there is a coupling of brimstone with fire, it is reasonable to suppose that sulfur dioxide, with its characteristic acrid odor, was usually meant. Brimstone in sacred writings designates the terrible and terrifying forces of nature used to execute the wrath of God.

History records that the Hebrews may have used brimstone to perpetrate a misrepresentation, for their ancient jewelry demonstrated a clever use of the mineral. Heavy gold bracelets were often cast hollow and filled with molten brimstone. Used partly to decrease weight, it also saved precious metal. No suggestion anywhere in Scriptural literature indicates that the Hebrews made really practical use of brimstone.

13. BRONZE

Bronze: an alloy, principally of copper and tin, with varying percentages of each metal.

. . . and when they come from the market place, they do not eat unless they purify themselves; and there are many other traditions which they observe, the washing of cups and pots and vessels of bronze. Mark 7:4, R.S.V.

Hammurabi (1728–1686 B.C.), the enlightened king, was the greatest ruler Babylonia ever had. He made remarkable achievements in his own country, but the world knows him because of the famous code of laws he originated. The Code of Hammurabi, composed more than 3,600 years ago, specifically mentioned bronze. One law states: "If a surgeon operates on a man with a bronze [knife] and the man gets well from a tumor or disease of the eye, the surgeon shall receive ten silver shekels. . . . If the man dies because the tumor is cut or the destruction of his eye, then the surgeon's hands shall be cut off." What a situation, and what a hazard, even for a modern surgeon!

Though native copper or its ores were not found in the confines of the Holy Land at the time that usage of the metal began, they were present in surrounding territories. The famous Gulf of Aqaba region in Edom did not become a part of the Holy Land proper until the time of Solomon (ca. 930–913 B.C.). These available copper ores had to be smelted and refined, as Job (28:2, R.S.V.)later commented. Through this smelting process it may have been accidentally discovered that if the copper was alloyed, particularly with tin, it achieved a spectacular hardness. So bronze was brought into being.

Bronze was in general use ages before the discovery of iron. Archaeologists have established that this alloy was made more than thirty centuries before Christ in the Indus Valley, Mesopotamia, and Egypt. The use of the metal became so widespread that it gave the name Bronze Age to a span of several millenniums during which the change from stone implements and weapons was made to the new metal. The Bronze Age began about 5,000 years ago. Excavation of abandoned mounds both east and west of the Jordan River, and the dating of distinctive pottery found there, has established fairly accurate dates for the different periods.

Early Bronze Age: ca. 3200–2100 B.C., the first historical era.

Middle Bronze Age: ca. 2100–1550 B.C., divided into Middle I and Middle II Ages.

Late Bronze Age: ca. 1550–1200 B.C., when Palestine was controlled by Egypt, followed by the first wave of the Hebrew conquest of Canaan.

The King James Version used the term "brass" for both copper and bronze, but modern translations render the word correctly. In Exodus 25, Moses is instructed to ask for offerings for the Tabernacle, and bronze is included with gold and silver (R.S.V.).

In following chapters, a listing of Tabernacle fixtures says: "Their pillars shall be twenty and their bases twenty, of bronze . . . and all the utensils of the tabernacle for every use . . . shall be of bronze" (Exod. 27:10, 19, R.S.V.).

While Solomon had untold riches and enormous resources, he lacked the skilled artisans necessary for the construction of the Temple. At his request, King Hiram of Tyre sent him: ". . . Huram-Abi, the son of a Danite woman, but his father was Tyrian, who knows how to work in gold, silver, bronze, iron, stone, and wood, in purple, violet, and fine linen, and in crimson, also to perform all manner of engraving and to sketch any artistic device that may be assigned to him, together with your skilled workmen and the skilled workmen of my Lord David, your father" (II Chron. 2:13–14, S.-G.). Tremendous pillars, the altar and its network (probably a grate on low feet), the basins and the "sea," animal figures and pomegranate decorations, all remarkably intricate, were cast by the highly skilled metalworker. ". . . even all these utensils which Hiram [Huram] made for King Solomon in the house of the Lord, were of burnished bronze" (I Kings 7:45, S.-G.).

Hiram poured the numerous bronze castings in clay molds in open ground between Succoth and Zarethan. The vessels were not weighed because of their numbers, so the weight of the bronze is not known

(I Kings 7:13–47, s.-g.). Dr. James B. Pritchard, leader of a University of Pennsylvania expedition, has found the place, on the Jordan Plain northeast of Jerusalem, where the bronze fittings for the Temple were cast, since he has recovered distinctive bronze artifacts from the area. He has identified the exact location of the ancient city Zarethan. In 587 b.c. King Nebuchadnezzar and his Chaldean host captured and pillaged Jerusalem. The victors broke into pieces the bronze pillars and bases and transported them to Babylon, along with the many Temple accouterments made of bronze. Israel's extension of the Bronze Age thus came to a tragic end.

An underseas expedition headed by Peter Throckmorton recently has found fine bronze specimens from an ancient wreck (rediscovered in 1966). A Roman ship was sunk in about the second century approximately 500 yards offshore in the Gulf of Taranto, on the south of Italy. Careful salvage yielded dozens of handmade bronze spikes, from four to ten inches long, like new, though submerged in salt water for seventeen centuries. Bronze coins and even a bronze shoulder strap from a Roman breastplate were recovered. Bronze artifacts have explained and virtually written many pages of history.

See Brass; Copper; Tin.

14. CARBUNCLE

Carbuncle: formerly referred to any one of several of the red precious stones, such as ruby; actually the garnet cut in rounded form (cabochon).

And thou shalt set in it settings of stones, even four rows of stones: the first row shall be a sardius, a topaz, and a carbuncle: this shall be the first row. Exodus 28:17, A.V.

Hidden deep within the dark-red heart of the garnet lie many ancient virtues attributed to no other gem. Its ages-old beauty is sustained by its enduring qualities of brilliance, fire, and hardness as well as its mystic symbolism. The garnet has been found in old-dynasty Egyptian talismans and even in New World Aztec votive offerings, and it had a legendary place in Aaron's breastplate. Once so rare that it was reserved for royalty, the garnet is now so easily obtained that any person can afford to wear the strikingly handsome stone and, if he wishes, believe in its good-luck-bringing attributes. This lovely, glowing stone, when cut in the rounded form, is the carbuncle of the ancients.

In the description of the high priest's breastplate we discover that a carbuncle is to be set in the first row of stones (the third). Here complications arise, for the word translated as carbuncle in the Authorized Version of the Bible should have been rendered "emerald," and conversely the word translated emerald should have been rendered "carbuncle." The Hebrew word *nōphĕk* means a shining stone, and it is difficult to understand why the King James scholars translated it as emerald. (*See* Emerald). Because it is one of the more plentiful gemstones, the garnet was probably the true carbuncle of the Bible, and there are several varieties that would qualify.

The word "carbuncle" derives from Latin and is a diminutive of *carbo*, meaning coal. The original root of the word "garnet" is the name "pomegranate," for the latter part of the term, *granum*, means a seed, and older civilizations seemed to see a very real resemblance between garnet gems and certain types of seeds. Though garnet has several color varieties, the almandite garnet, popularly known as almandine, is one of the most beautiful garnets and has been a favorite for many centuries. The name of almandine is an alteration of the name of Alabanda, an ancient city in Asia Minor where the carbuncles of Pliny's time were cut and polished. A favorite of Roman engravers, the almandite garnet was carved into beautiful intaglios and cameos. One of the finest intaglios ever made is the "Head of the Dog Sirius," in the Marlborough collection.

The deep, clear-red, glowing color of this gem (owing in great part to the inclusion of ferric iron) lends credence to the old Hebrew legend which tells that a large carbuncle was hung in the ark and that it supplied plenteous light to all the voyagers within the craft. The basis for this account may be in an ancient Hebrew word once used for carbuncle that literally meant "lighting a fire."

Other varieties of garnet make brilliantly beautiful gems, and certainly some of these must have been known and used by ancient peoples. Pyrope, named for the Greek word meaning "fiery," has an especially fine red color, like dancing sparks. The spessartite, red with a brownish to golden tinge, may have been unknown, as it is relatively rare. The grossularite series of golden brown, orange, and reddish brown, respectively kown as cinnamon stone (hessonite), hyacinth-garnet, and jacinth-garnet, was undoubtedly familiar in the older eras. Here again, centuries-old names have come down to modern times, and one wonders whether the terms "jacinth" and "hyacinth" actually referred to garnets or to zircons in olden cultures. It is interesting to speculate, too, how peoples of those times regarded the green-colored garnets, the grossularite gooseberry shade, and the brilliant, vivid green of the demantoid, a variety of andradite garnet. In all probability these were classed as emeralds, for that term seems to have included all the similar green-hued gemstones. The Uralian emerald of more recent years is an especially beautiful garnet of nearly emerald-green color. It was discovered in the Ural Mountains.

In modern times most garnets are faceted, as cutting them in such style intensifies the glowing color, but the typical red gem has been cut in the ancient manner for more than 2,000 years, resulting in a smooth, rounded top surface, called *cabochon*. This was the true carbuncle!

Distributed widely over the world, garnets of large size and deep color come from Fort Wrangell, Alaska. Other localities in the United States include Mason's Branch, Macon County, North Carolina, where rose-colored garnets are found, and Ruby Mountain, Nathrop, Colorado, where fine dark-red crystals occur in rhyolite.

15. CARNELIAN (CORNELIAN)

Carnelian: a reddish variety of chalcedony without crystal form but under the microscope shows a fibrous structure.

The foundations of the wall of the city were adorned with every jewel; . . . the sixth carnelian. . . . *Revelation 21:19–20, R.S.V.*

Modern woman, with her love of bright gems, emulates her sisters of ancient days. Outside the thick fortified walls of an Iron Age city about 3,000 years old, an ancient cemetery of the same period had been uncovered. In the plot was an elaborate tomb, one of the finest ever found in Jordan. The tomb held the skeleton of a regal lady, perhaps a queen. A necklace more than ten feet long was found adorning the skeleton. Contained in the necklace were 670 orange-red carnelian beads, along with 72 beads of gold. This exciting discovery was announced recently by Dr. James B. Pritchard, the leader of a team of archaeologists excavating Tell es-Sa'idiyeh (Zarethan) in the Jordan River Valley, northeast of Jerusalem.

Other excavations of a much older period, by Leonard Woolley in 1922 at Ur of Sumer (or "of the Chaldees"), brought to light the royal tombs, in which Queen Shub-ad, her consort, and sixty-eight ladies had been buried about 2500 B.C. A delicate filigree cape of polished gold, decorated with carnelian, lapis lazuli, and assorted beads, almost covered the remains of the queen. Around her throat was a collar necklace of gold, with alternating triangles of carnelian and lapis lazuli.

A string of expertly etched carnelian beads, dating back to 3100 B.C., was recovered in Egypt. Other Egyptian antiquities attest the lavish use of carnelian, for King Tutankhamen's casket holding the mummy (the inner one of four cases) was of beaten gold, lavishly encrusted with turquoise, lapis lazuli, and carnelian. The New York Metropolitan Museum of Art possesses a fabulous headdress of a lady of the court of Thutmos III which is made of gold inlaid with carnelian and glass.

In the five widely used Bible versions, carnelian—occasionally spelled "cornelian" and also called sardius—is given as the sixth gem ornamenting the foundation stones of the New Jerusalem (Rev. 21:20), and Smith-Goodspeed and the Confraternity Version list it as the first breastplate stone in place of sardius. Technically there is no difference between these gems. Sardius, like carnelian, is a color variety of chalcedony, emphasizing brown shades rather than red. Mineralogically, carnelian is a fibrous-structured variety of quartz in which hematite is the probable source of the distinguishing red color. Carnelian's name might have come from the Latin *corneus*, meaning fleshy, because of the color.

Carnelian takes a high, lustrous polish to which wax will not readily adhere, a quality that made it especially desirable for seals. It was often used for scarabs, some of which served a dual purpose. The flat reverse side of the scarab was engraved with the owner's name and appropriate symbols. Swivel rings were made by drilling the scarab lengthwise, inserting a wire through the center, and fastening the wire to the shanks of the finger band so the setting could pivot. A simple movement turned the amulet so that it also served as a signet or seal.

Carnelian is susceptible to heat treatment. A dull, unattractive red may be changed, by heating, to a desirable, vivid, orange-red hue. Usually translucent, and often described as flesh-red, fine carnelian is nearer being a tomato or Chinese red, similar to the color of the famous Chinese lacquer. A good, well-colored, flawless carnelian is somewhat of a rarity.

In remote times India undoubtedly furnished much gem rough, but the great Egyptian and Arabian deserts were also sources of excellent material. It is theorized that long exposure to the sun deepened the color of the surface finds, for specimens dug at some depth in the same desert areas always show much lighter hues.

Brazil produces high-grade carnelian; in our country, in the Far West, particularly Washington, Idaho, Nevada, Oregon, and California, numerous specimens of gem quality have been found. A bright red stone found in the Utah desert south of Cisco, locally called pigeon-blood agate, is in reality a carnelian. Carnelian has been reported from the Tampa Bay area, Florida.

See Sardine Stone; Sardius; Sardonyx.

16. CHALCEDONY

Chalcedony: a translucent to transparent cryptocrystalline variety of quartz with a waxy luster; usually very light-colored, white, grayish, and pale blue; is regarded as cryptocrystalline because the indistinct crystal grains cannot be discerned without the aid of a microscope.

And the foundations of the wall of the city were garnished with all manner of precious stones. The first foundation was jasper . . . the third, a chalcedony. . . . Revelation 21:19, A.V.

"Cooking or boiling chalcedonies and agates in honey deepens and intensifies the coloring of the stone," a craftsman in gems might once have advised his apprentice. In ancient Egypt, this craft was practiced to improve the quality of poor stones. Long ago, Egyptian artisans discovered that chalcedony and agate were somewhat porous and would absorb liquids. This was probably the first successful "doctoring" of chalcedony and similar gemstones. The Germans, in the past century, developed this artificial coloring to a point reaching perfection. Staining chalcedony to give it more attractive colors has been done to imitate more desirable gems. In this way imitation "chrysoprase" or blue "lapis lazuli" has been produced from ordinary pale chalcedony.

Chalcedony, a cryptocrystalline variety of quartz, is a mosaic of microscopic crystalline grains forming a compact, flinty aggregate. Not suitable for faceting, it is always cut in cabochon form for gems. Some authorities have grouped all varieties of cryptocrystalline quartz under the heading of the chalcedony family, but common usage designates the milky-white, light gray, blue, and yellowish-brown stones as chalcedony and gives the descriptive names of carnelian, bloodstone, agate, etc., to those gemstones of distinctive color and pattern.

Chalcedony, like agate, is usually found in volcanic rocks, deeply hidden in the dark recesses of the long-cooled lava. It was deposited there by circulating groundwaters carrying quantities of silicon dioxide in solution. The coloring is due to traces of other elements, such as iron, present in the groundwater as it worked its way through the rock.

June Culp Zeitner, a contributing editor of the *Lapidary Journal*, recently described a peculiar find of chalcedony in Star County, Texas. She found the pieces of chalcedony, which she named "icicles," in vertical positions in hot clay banks. When removed, they were icy clear or blue gray with a white icy coating and cool to the touch. Pale in color and fragile when freshly dug, after being allowed to "cure," they were very hard and took a lovely polish.

The Greek word *chalkedōn* in indicative of our modern, light-colored chalcedony. The Greek term *iaspis*, usually translated "jasper," seemingly included, from Pliny's description, a number of varieties of delicately colored, translucent quartz (chalcedony) in addition to the familiar darker-hued stones. If Pliny was correct, chrysoprase could be included, and though not a quartz mineral variety, jade may have been included in Pliny's description.

The account in Revelation 21:20 says that the third stone garnishing the foundation walls was chalcedony. Much of the material called chalcedony in ancient times may have been milky quartz, given that appearance by innumerable microscopic liquid inclusions. But the true distinctive chalcedony was found at Chalcedon, in Bithynia, from which locality it got its name. This area probably supplied a major portion of the chalcedony used by the people of Israel.

Chalcedony was abundantly used for carving seals for identification and communication. Seals performed a little-recognized but important service in disseminating many secrets of the arts. Contrary to popular belief, these secrets were not passed by word of mouth or hand to hand, but they traveled with these little objects of trade, seals. They illustrated craftsmen of all kinds going about their trades and details of daily life and the dress of many cultures. The tiniest of all were the diminutive seals of translucent chalcedony and agate. Upon them were carved miniature scenes, done with delicate touch and incredible skill—scenes depicting suppliants kneeling before enthroned deities; a warrior astride a horse, in mortal combat with a savage animal; or tamed animals standing beside the Tree of Life, protected and shielded by guardian spirits.

Chalcedony was reputed to have the power to drive away bad dreams and was, in primitive days, supposed to be good for ailments of the eyes. It was much used for intaglios. A favorite carving was the image of a man with his right hand raised aloft, which, it was believed, gave success to the wearer when involved in a law suit. One wonders about the integrity of law courts in those days, if litigants resorted to the use of such charms! In the Middle Ages, chalcedony symbolized the pure flame of inner chastity and zeal for truth.

Today chalcedony is a favorite stone of the lapidary fraternity. Found all over the United States in many lovely colors, it is still a treasured semiprecious gem.

See Agate; Carnelian; Sardius.

17. CHALK (CHALKSTONES)

Chalk: a very soft limestone, white, gray, or buff in color, usually composed of the fossil shells of ancient sea inhabitants.

By this therefore shall the iniquity of Jacob be purged; and this is all the fruit to take away his sin; when he maketh all the stones of the altar as chalkstones that are beaten in sunder, the groves and images shall not stand up. *Isaiah 27:9, A.V.*

The Wadi el Afranj, in the neighborhood of Beit Jibrin, is a reminder of the Crusaders. The Knights of St. John built a church and fortifications here which consequently gave the wadi its name, Valley of the Franks. Far below the Judean highlands, this area has tremendous deposits of yellow chalk. The place is also an early center of Christianity, but the converts paid a horrible price in the persecutions under Diocletian and Maximin. Many hid from Roman authorities by taking refuge in the caves of the chalk ridges.

Although many of these caverns were natural, others were man-made, for the yellow chalk was easy to carve and hardened on exposure to the atmosphere. Some caves appear to have been Jewish tombs, but many had pillared halls, connecting staircases, and long corridors with niches for lamps. Practically the only motif used in decorations found on the walls was the cross. Frequently the entrances are low passages along which a person has to creep or crawl, suggesting that they originated in times of terror.

In the Authorized Version there is only one mention of chalkstone or chalk that we have discovered: ". . . he maketh all the stones of the altar as chalkstones that are beaten in sunder . . ." (Isa. 27:9). *The Jerusalem Bible*, however, in describing the making of an idol, suggests a common usage of chalk not found in other widely used versions: "The wood carver takes his measurements, outlines the image with chalk, carves it with chisels" (Isa. 44:13).

Chalk, in association with limestone and dolomite, makes up the carbonate group of sedimentary rocks. Chalk is present in quantity, being carried in solution by freshwater streams; but because it is relatively insoluble in seawater, it is quickly deposited after reaching the sea. Either through the life processes of marine organisms or by the direct precipitation of calcium carbonate, the mineral calcite settles to the sea floor as extremely fine-grained calcareous mud. If this is compacted into rock, yet remains soft and porous, it is chalk.

Some authorities believe the term "chalkstone" in the Hebrew literally means "stones of boiling," and thus "stones of lime," or limestone. However, the word "chalk" or "plaster" in Greek is *gypsus*, from which gypsum gets its name. Gypsum is hydrous calcium sulfate, a common salt which precipitates when a body of seawater is cut off from the ocean, or when a lake has no outlet and evaporates in a dry climate. Plaster is made from rock gypsum, which is found in extensive bedded deposits in almost every country. Palestine has large deposits of both limestone and gypsum, the latter being found in some parts of the Jordan Valley. Thus raw material which could be treated for making mortar, plaster, or stucco was readily available. Limestone requires intense heat and large amounts of fuel to release carbon dioxide gas and pulverize it to a usable form, and fuel was never plentiful in the Holy Land. Gypsum could be fired at a much lower temperature, requiring less fuel, and made an enduring plaster for use in the semidesert climate. So the Biblical allusion to chalkstone may have meant gypsum.

The use of gypsum for plaster can be traced back to antiquity, for it was known to the Egyptians 5,000 years ago. It was freely used, with colors, for interior wall paintings which were overlaid with varnish. It was also utilized to make plaster for the Egyptian pyramids. Plaster of some sort, though it may have been a heavy whitewash or a fine mortar made of lime, was used as a lining for cisterns and tombs throughout the East. Gutters or drainage channels of cement fed the cisterns during rainy periods, and the material of which this cement was made is still hard and waterproof after 3,000 years.

The Hebrews knew and used plaster. Ezekiel tells of the Lord's displeasure with false prophets who spoke with "empty words and lying visions." "Since they have misled my people by saying: Peace! when there is no peace. Instead of my people rebuilding the wall, these men come and slap on plaster" (Ezek 13:10, J.B.)

In remote times, the method of treating both limestone and gypsum was to dig a saucer-like depression or pit three or four feet deep. In this were piled alternate layers of brushwood and the mineral, broken into small pieces by a wheel similar to that of an oil press. The brush was then kindled, and the burning material covered by dirt and sod. An aperture was left open for draft, much as was done in the ancient charcoal heaps. Today when gypsum is made into plaster it is "burned," that is, it is heated gently to a temperature a little above 212 degrees Fahrenheit in order to drive off three-fourths of the contained water. When powdered, this is the familiar plaster of Paris. When plaster of Paris is mixed with water, regaining its lost moisture, it makes a quick-setting plaster, a firm recrystallized material.

Familiar to everyone are the chalk crayons used on schoolroom blackboards. Chalk, free from impurities, is soft, porous, and lacking in grit. Much of it was used for decades for writing purposes, but now the material in blackboard crayons is a manufactured product made from burned gypsum, not chalk at all.

See Lime.

18. CHRYSOLITE

Chrysolite (with peridot): gem of the mineral olivine; compound of magnesium, iron, silica, and oxygen; transparent crystals or grains cut lovely gemstones.

And the foundations of the wall of the city were garnished with all manner of precious stones . . . the seventh, chrysolyte. *Revelation 21:19–20, A.V.*

Often there is a strange confounding of the names of Bible gems, and one of the most amazing and confusing is the use of the name "topaz" for chrysolite. Conversely, chrysolite was the name for topaz. The use of these gem names in reversed order persisted for many centuries after Bible times. In the sixteenth century writers still used "topaz" to refer to peridot, gem olivine, but more green in hue than chrysolite.

Pliny described chrysolite as having its own highly prized shade of green, being priced above all other stones when first found. He mentions two varieties of the gem: *prasoides,* which was the true peridot, and *chrysopteron* (chrysolite), which strongly resembled chrysoprasus. Aware of its lack of hardness and that the stone wore badly with use, he said it was polished with an iron file, whereas all other gems required emery stone.

Pliny quoted Archelaus (fifth century B.C.), who claimed the gems came from a Red Sea Island called Chitis. Pirates, driven by adverse winds, were compelled to land on the inhospitable island. Nearly starved, they dug roots and herbs to subsist, and in the digging, found topazos (chrysolite). Though Pliny spelled the island's name Topazos, it is more often spelled Topazios. Topazios has been identified as a small, triangular island 34 miles off the coast of Egypt in the Red Sea, now called St. John's Island or Zeberged. It is the world's principal locality for gem peridot, but topaz has never been found on the island.

An old legend tells that the inhabitants of this island used the gemstones as currency to pay their tribute to Egyptian rulers. They believed that topazos could be found only at night, when it was said to give out a radiance like the sun. Though the gemstone was believed to glow, it was never mined at night, but the spot where it shone was carefully marked. The gem seekers would return in daylight to dig up the treasured stones.

The peridot deposits were discovered and mining begun between 1580 and 1350 B.C., and they are still occasionally mined. Lamps and vases found on the island indicate that gem mining was carried on during the Greek domination of Egypt, but positive evidence of earlier intensive mining is lacking.

Chrysolite is a gem variety of the mineral olivine which gets its name from the typical olive-green color. One of its types of occurrence is in basic igneous rocks formed by the crystallization of magmas low in silica and rich in magnesia or in lavas, both extrusive and intrusive types. Here olivine is found in somewhat crystalline grains or aggregates and at times as large well-formed crystals. It is also found as granular masses in volcanic bombs, in Germany and Arizona. New Zealand's Dun Mountain, a whole mountain made up of large masses of olivine, has given its name to a rock composed almost entirely of olivine, dunite. North Carolina also has very large masses of olivine.

In Arizona and New Mexico olivine grains weathered out of ancient lava flows were later buried under drifting sands. Reservation Indians gather gemlike particles from large anthills and sell them to collectors and tourists. Industrious ants have brought these to the surface from underground. Because of their pitted appearance, they are locally called Job's tears.

Imbedded grains of chrysolite are also found in meteorites. Dr. George Frederick Kunz, famed gemmologist, tells of one-carat peridots he obtained from meteoric iron found in Santa Fe County, New Mexico. (A gem cut of material from space would be a fascinating conversation piece.)

The confusion in naming the gem is further confounded because the Greek name of chrysolite literally means "gold stone." The term was meant to include all yellow-hued stones, such as the yellow beryls (heliodor) and some zircons. Perhaps the golden topaz would have been in that classification, as well as yellow quartz, called citrine. A. Paul Davis selected golden citrine as the second stone of the first row in his replica of the breastplate as shown in the frontispiece. The Moffatt translation gives this second stone as chrysolite.

Chrysolite and peridot are quite soft gems, too soft to be satisfactory ring stones, and should be worn only in a type of jewelry that is protected from abrasion. Some peridots, the greener-hued olivine gems found on the jewelry market today, are stones recut from those taken to Europe by Crusaders who believed they were emeralds. Church treasuries of Europe often contained stones they thought were emeralds. The so-called emeralds of the "Three Magi" in the Cathedral of Cologne are not emeralds, but peridots, though their source is unknown. The finest color of chrysolite or peridot is a beautiful bottle green, which has caused it to be called "evening emerald." Recently some crystals made available in America were quickly and eagerly purchased by admirers of the ancient gem.

See Topaz.

19. CHRYSOPRASE (CHRYSOPRASUS)

Chrysoprase: a rather rare, apple-green variety of chalcedony; when brilliant, is highly valued and makes desirable gems.

And the foundations of the wall of the city were garnished with all manner of precious stones. The first foundation was jasper; . . . the tenth, a chrysoprasus. *Revelation* 21:19–20, A.V.

Many large gemstones are known, but it is unusual to find furniture made of a gem material. In the Old Palace at Potsdam, Frederick the Great of Prussia had it used lavishly. Two tables of chrysoprase, each three feet in length and two feet in width, are among the impressive objects seen there.

Used as a gem, chrysoprase has been exquisitely carved into cameos. One, six by five inches, is carved from a single piece of gem-quality material. This lovely second-century engraving, believed to be the largest chrysoprase gem, depicts the head of the Roman god Jupiter. The cameo is a valued piece in the superb Maxwell-Summerville Collection, at the University of Pennsylvania, which contains more than 2,000 engraved gems from all over the world, including ancient seals, signets, talismans, and carved pieces of many civilizations.

As with many gems, chrysoprase was admired and used by ancient peoples. An Egyptian mummy of about 1500 B.C., adorned with a stunning necklace which included beads of chrysoprase, has been discovered.

The name is derived from two Greek words: *chrusos*, signifying gold, and *prason*, the leek, in reference to the predominant shades of color in the stone. The stone chrysoprase, of seawater or hoarhound green, resembled the green juice of the leek. The color is ascribed to nickel oxide, so the gem material is usually found in the vicinity of deposits of nickel minerals. Since nickel is often present, if only in minute amounts, in many rock types, it is possible for percolating groundwater to dissolve out the nickel, which is then deposited with the silica in the crystallization of the chalcedonic quartz, giving it the leek-green color.

The famous deposits of chrysoprase in Silesia were exhausted more than a century ago, making the gem rare and somewhat extensively imitated by dyeing other quartz materials. Nickel in sizable deposits is scarce in the United States, which explains the relative scarcity of chrysoprase in this country. Recent discoveries of this mineral in California and Oregon eased the situation slightly, but the amount of gem material found has been disappointing. Superb gem chrysoprase is presently being imported from Australia.

According to Dr. George Frederick Kunz, Tiffany's noted gem expert, chrysoprase was once thought to have strange and wonderful powers as a talisman. During the Middle Ages it was generally believed that if a thief condemned to be hanged or beheaded placed this stone in his mouth, he would escape the just punishment for his crimes. Just how this could happen was never stated, but in some way the stone was supposed to make the condemned invisible, and thus he could escape the executioner.

In the Authorized Version of the Scriptures the only reference to chrysoprasus, meaning our modern chrysoprase, is in the listing of the stones of the foundation of the New Jerusalem (Rev. 21:20). The other commonly used versions of the Bible name jasper as the twelfth stone of the breastplate of the high priest (except the Moffatt translation), and A. Paul Davis selected chrysoprase as this stone (see frontispiece). Since we believe the jasper of the breastplate may have been jade, usually considered a green gem, the green of chrysoprase may have been a very reasonable choice.

20. CLAY

Clay: an earthy material, plastic when moist but hard when dry and even harder when baked or fired; much of it comes from the disintegration of solid minerals such as the feldspars.

He brought me up also out of an horrible pit, out of the miry clay, and set my feet upon a rock, and established my goings. Psalm 40:2, A.V.

A library of 22,000 volumes may seem small to us—many of our libraries contain 250,000 or more. However, this library is a very special one. It is the famous library of King Ashurbanipal, uncovered at ancient Nineveh, and the books are clay tablets or cylinders. Although Ashurbanipal built his library about 650 B.C., some of the clay tablets it housed date back to the great Babylonian King Hammurabi, the law-giver of 1728–1686 B.C. An epic poem of 300 quatrains is one of the oldest books. Inscribed on twelve clay tablets, it relates the Babylonian version of the Flood.

Only one other discovery of clay cylinders and tablets exceeds Ashurbanipal's astounding library. At Mari, on the Euphrates River, a magnificent palace covering more than ten acres was unearthed. Cuneiform writings on hardened clay were found in many rooms, totaling almost 25,000 tablets and cylinders dating back to about 3000 B.C.

What a debt modern man owes to clay! Through its ancient use much knowledge has been preserved. Some tablets used for personal correspondence reveal details of daily life in previously unknown cultures. Police reports from distant outposts, lists of craftsmen, and details of merchandise received and sold were found inscribed at Mari. Information about gods, religious ceremonies and festivals, and the old Chaldean traditions of the creation, the fall of man, and the deluge have been preserved on clay. Babylonian and Assyrian scribes kept accounts showing tax payments and other transactions as early as 2500 B.C. To preserve them, the clay sheets were baked after being inscribed.

Clay is the basis for all pottery, and pottery-making goes back to the very beginnings of civilizations. From even very small remnants of pottery, archaeologists are able to date the occupants of an area or a culture within a century or less. In 1890, Sir Flinders Petrie, noted archaeologist, worked out "the yardstick of pottery" with its "sequence dating" by comparing bits of clay with pottery already dated from other lands and cultures. In his excavations at Tell el Hesī in South Judea, Petrie explored 2,000 years of history in six weeks by studying the pottery shards found in the many "layers" of occupation at the mound.

By numerous passages referring to pottery and its manufacture, the Bible indicates that it was an important craft in ancient days, and that the makers of the clay vessels were valued highly. "These were the potters and inhabitants of Netaim and Gederah; they dwelt there with the king for his work" (1 Chron. 4:23, R.S.V.). Although the former place is unknown, the latter is located in the Judean lowlands. The potters mentioned, attached to the royal household, are listed in the official genealogy of Judah that is preserved in First Chronicles. These artisans were descendants of Shelah, the son of Judah. Here archaeologists have discovered stamped jar handles verifying that these were royal potters who worked for the king.

Pottery-making was a well-developed art in Bible times, and the use of wheels and the casting of clay upon the wheel are described, but with few details regarding molding or the specific vessels made.

> *It is so with the potter, as he sits at his work,*
> *And turns the wheel with his foot;*
> *He is constantly careful about his work,*
> *And all his manufacture is by measure;*
> *He will shape the clay with his arm,*
> *And bend its strength with his feet;*
> *He puts his mind on finishing the glazing,*
> *And he is anxious to make his furnace clean.*
>
> (Ecclus. 38:29–30, s.-g., the Apocrypha)

Many references are made to the potter's control over his clay as symbolic of God's control over the destiny of mankind, and the failure of clay and metal to fuse as a figurative example.

Pottery's widespread household use is often described, as is the use of pottery in the Temple sacrifices. The Scriptures define what made pottery unclean so that it had to be discarded and broken. Pottery shards were used "to take fire from the hearth," and they replaced cups to dip water from a pool. Pottery clay was used in the Middle East, and still is, for sealing jars and closing doors, even those of sepulchers.

At Petra a unique ancient use of pottery came to light. Modern engineers planned to make the colorful ruins, in the southwestern desert of the modern kingdom of Jordan, safe from flash floods. They found it feasible to restore stone dams which had diverted water into storage basins, later drained for irrigation. The Nabataean founders had built the city's dams about 300 B.C. These builders of Petra were a step ahead of the Romans. They used pottery pipes to carry the water instead of aqueducts!

Each excavation reveals more about life in days of antiquity. The first known bathtub dates back about 3,600 years, to the palace of King Minos of Crete. Made of painted clay, shaped much like today's tub, it had terra cotta piping.

J. Jordan and C. Preusser, archaeologists of a German expedition sent out by the Deutsche Orient-Gesellschaft in the early 1900's, made some thorough excavations at Uruk (ancient Erech) in Mesopotamia. They found very remarkable wall decorations of about 3200 B.C. Massive walls and columns of sun-dried, plaster-covered brick were discovered. Ornamental vivid mosaic patterns had been formed by driving baked clay nails with colored heads into the plaster.

The lavish retreat of King Herod, Masada (built 36–35 B.C., at a time when Herod feared both the Jews' and Cleopatra's designs on Judea), was complete with a casemate wall around the perimeter, towers for defense, vast underground cisterns to catch rain diverted there by aqueducts, storehouses containing bountiful stocks of food and unworked metals, arsenals of many kinds of weapons, and court palaces. Though Roman soldiers occupied it after Herod's death, Jewish rebels captured and held it until A.D. 73, using it as headquarters for their guerrilla warfare against the Romans.

Pottery fragments helped reveal the dramatic and tragic story of the Jewish Zealots who died at Masada the night of April 15, A.D. 73. After seven years of revolt, their mountain fortress was smashed by Roman battering rams and set afire. Morning revealed the bodies of most of the band of 960 rebels who had decided their own fate. Each man destroyed his own family; then, drawing lots made of potsherd, they killed one another, the last man taking his own life.

Archaeologists have excavated and partially restored Masada, which is located in stark and desolate desert land. The massive plateau, somewhat boat-shaped, about a half-mile long and an eighth of a mile wide, has sheer walls which drop abruptly 1,300 feet to the shores of the Dead Sea. Yigael Yadin, Israeli archaeologist, who directed this largest of digs in the Middle East, reports that the most exciting discoveries were not related to clay, but to the fragments of scrolls, fourteen in number, including parts of Genesis, Leviticus, Deuteronomy, Psalms, and Ezekiel, which are identical with the text and spelling of the traditional Hebrew Bible. A copy of the lost Hebrew original of Ecclesiasticus (the Apocrypha) was found, and a fragment of a long-lost Hebrew original of the Book of Jubilees was discovered. Most exciting of all was the location of a portion of a scroll identical to fragments of one of the Dead Sea Scrolls from Qumran. In addition to these finds, more than 700 ostraka (inscribed potsherds) were discovered, including eleven small pieces, each bearing a different name. One wonders if these are related to the lots drawn by the men in the destruction of one another after taking the lives of their band.

The Hebrews used many materials in their building, though ordinary houses and similar buildings were of bricks made by mixing clay with chopped barley or wheat straw, and sun-dried. Everyone is familiar with the poignant story of the Hebrews in Egypt, forced to make bricks without straw being furnished to them. (Straw was necessary to keep the bricks from cracking as they dried under the hot sun.) The picture is starkly drawn in Exodus: "That same day, Pharaoh gave this command to the people's slave-drivers and to the overseers. Up to the present, you have provided these people with straw for brickmaking. Do so no longer; let them go and gather straw for themselves" (5:6–7, J.B.). The hard, forced labor of the Israelites in the brickyards and the inhumane demands of the Egyptian ruler and his henchmen are related in the story.

In Nahum's time, about 612 B.C., the primitive practice of treading clay was still in use. At the same time, the use of the brick kiln is mentioned, indicating bricks were fired rather than hardened in the sun. "Draw thee waters for the siege, fortify thy strong holds: go into clay, and tread the mortar, make strong the brickkiln" (Nah. 3:14, A.V.).

The art of brickmaking was understood and practiced by all ancient cultures. Details of processes are mentioned in Egyptian inscriptions and graphically illustrated on the walls of their tombs and temples.

Clay had a strange, revealing use in the New World. Tiny clay figures, a thousand or more years old, have been found in ancient graves, molded and placed there by ancient Indian sculptors of South America and Mexico. The figures had been molded to indicate the ailment causing the death of the person buried. Dark splotches on a face and parts of the nose and lips missing indicate leprosy or some similar tropical disease. Bone deformities and injuries are unmistakably shown.

21. COAL

Coal: in the Bible, probably not the prehistoric plant and tree deposits changed by pressure and heat to the mineral coal as modern man knows it, but more likely charcoal made by charring wood in a kiln, with the air excluded.

Then flew one of the seraphims unto me, having a live coal in his hand, which he had taken with the tongs from off the altar. *Isaiah 6:6, A.V.*

Stones that burn! How amazed must have been the man who first made that discovery. Yet history gives us no clue as to when and where it happened. Theophrastus, the Greek philosopher, in about 300 B.C. wrote about mineral coal, since he compares it to charcoal.

The "stone that burns" helped start man up the long road of civilization.

Coal is more widely used than any other natural resource, despite the importance of copper, tin, sulfur, petroleum, and other minerals so urgently needed by our modern industries. More than 2,000 useful products are made from this remarkable material, without which the refining of iron and steel is impossible. Paradoxically, coal furnishes both heat and cold, for it yields ammonia, extensively used in some refrigerating and icemaking methods. Neoprene, one of the best artificial rubbers, is a product of coal. Where natural petroleum supplies are scant, gasoline is distilled from coal. Coal tar derivatives run the gamut in producing useful products for man, from flavorings and perfumes to tear gas and insecticides, including dyes, preservatives, plastics, synthetic textiles, and even medicine such as aspirin and sulfa drugs. It is also the source of tremendous energy, being used in some areas as the fuel for producing electricity.

In our English Bible, the term "coal" represents five different Hebrew words. Not one of the five means mineral coal. Isaiah mentions the smith blowing upon the coals, doubtless charcoal, and roasting meat upon coals of fire. Psalm 140 uses falling, burning coals as a symbol of punishment, and in II Samuel 14:7 a young mother refers to her remaining son as "my coal which is left." In other instances coal means heated rocks which are placed in a closed oven, providing heat for baking. Similar methods are still used by some Pueblo Indians in the southwestern United States.

There is no proof that the Hebrews ever used mineral coal. There are no deposits of true coal in the Holy Land, though there are occurrences in Lebanon, which the knowledgeable Phoenicians perhaps used. The Hebrews may also have known of this source, but they could hardly have imported the material for their own use. Other fuel was nearer, cheaper, and easier to get.

In ancient times, when Palestine was plentifully forested, wood was the common fuel. Many Biblical references to coal meant charcoal, and the Psalms and the Book of Job tell of some sources of wood for charcoal, such as rushes, thorns, and the broom shrub, which reputedly provided the best.

Charcoal, with incense added, was burned in the priestly censers. It was the fuel used in smelting precious metals. Kilns fired by charcoal were used for the baking of pottery and brick. The "burning fiery furnace" may have been a large, perpendicular, hollow shaft with an opening at the base for the removal of plaster (calcined gypsum).

One Biblical proverb uses the figurative expression "heaping coals of fire on an enemy's head," representing the shame and confusion men feel when their evildoing is requited by good. "If thine enemy be hungry give him bread to eat; and if he be thirsty give him water to drink: For thou shalt heap coals of fire upon his head . . ." (Prov. 25:21–22, A.V.). Such an expression may have had a very practical meaning. Household fires, if unattended, will go out. Without matches, flint and tinder would be necessarily used in the tedious process of kindling it again. An alternative would be to borrow live coals from a nearby householder. Placed in an earthenware vessel, they would be carried upon the head. How easy to carry out the Biblical injunction by giving a spiteful neighbor a generous supply of burning coals to rekindle his home fire!

One variety of true coal definitely known to the people of Bible times never burned. Jet! A hard, glossy, dense, black gem-coal, jet had been used for jewelry and ornamentation for at least a millennium before Christ. The best-known source was at what is now Whitby, England, where mines were producing it as early as 1500 B.C. Romans worked the mines, sending the product home in Caesar's time, for jet spangles and buttons have been found in ruins of Roman dwellings of that period. Jet is sometimes known as "black amber," a most appropriate name when the similar organic origin of the two gem minerals is considered.

Dr. George Frederick Kunz has said that jet from El Paso County, Colorado, rivals the finest known and that Trinchera Mesa, Wet Mountain Valley, Colorado, and many coal seams in the state yield jet.

22. COPPER

Copper: a common metallic element, reddish in color, that is readily bent, easily extended, yet tough; one of the best conductors of heat and electricity.

For the Lord your God is bringing you into a good land, . . . a land whose stones are iron, and out of whose hills you can dig copper. Deuteronomy 8:7, 9, R.S.V.

Not many years ago a copper artifact of Bible times posed a perplexing problem to archaeologists. The object was one of the Dead Sea Scrolls. Nearly everyone knows the story of the exciting discovery of these scrolls in 1947 by Bedouin shepherds in isolated caves in the precipitous slopes near this salty sea. In 1952 two adjacent caves were explored, and further finds were made. Among the newfound scrolls was a copper one that could not be unrolled because of its oxidized condition. It was a long, narrow sheet of metal, beaten paper-thin, with ancient characters impressed in it. Later a second copper scroll was found, but it also was too brittle to be unrolled like the other scrolls, which were of papyrus or leather.

How to learn the contents of these copper scrolls? How to unroll them without breaking them into innumerable, undecipherable fragments? Professor H. W. Baker, of Manchester University in England, developed a plan to cut these priceless scrolls into readable segments. By the use of a tiny, revolving saw, operated under a powerful magnifying glass, he was able to separate one scroll into nineteen slices, much like slicing a jelly roll the wrong way. By extraordinary good fortune, not one single letter was lost in this delicate cutting operation, although about 5 percent of the letters were missing because of breaks and deterioration of the copper through the many centuries. It was found that the two scrolls were one scroll which had been broken when the Essene writers rolled the copper sheet imperfectly.

The scroll describes more than fifty separate hidden treasure hoards— all within fifty miles or so of the Dead Sea. But the passing centuries have obliterated most of the identifying landmarks, and it is significant that metal came out a poor second in lasting qualities when compared to organic paper and leather. And copper has always been considered an imperishable metal!

Such references as " . . . two vessels of fine copper, precious as gold" (Ezra 28:26–27) are few in the King James Version. Translators of the seventeenth century used the word "brass" for either copper or bronze. In many cases the context indicates that copper is definitely meant, while in others the allusion is distinctly to the alloy bronze.

Surely the phrase "a land whose stones are iron, and out of whose hills thou mayest dig brass" (Deut. 8:9, A.V.) refers to copper and its mining. Is there any doubt that Goliath's armor was bronze when one reads the description of it: "And he had a helmet of brass upon his head, and he was armed with a coat of mail; and the weight of the coat was five thousand shekels of brass. And he had greaves of brass upon his legs, and a target of brass between his shoulders" (I Sam. 17:5–6, A.V.)?

In the Near East copper was used as early as 4500 to 4000 B.C. at the start of the Stone-Copper Age, also called the Chalcolithic Age (ca. 4500–3000 B.C.). The oldest of all the evidence yet found of the use of copper intruding into the age of stone implements, dating perhaps to the end of the fifth millennium B.C., is that discovered at Jericho VIII, a stratum excavated in the city so ancient that it may be one of the oldest sites not only in Palestine but in the world. Certainly Jericho is the oldest fortified town known, and flints found there in association with other remains date it back to the ninth or eighth millennium B.C. The exciting finds at Jericho were made by Dr. Kathleen M. Kenyon of the British School of Archaeology. Mesopotamia's Halaf culture may have used copper as early as 4000 B.C., and slowly its use spread westward to the Mediterranean.

Archaeologists have found copper objects at ancient Troy, and even the stone bowls used in casting them. Copper nails were cast in Assyria at least as early as 1700 B.C., and in Egypt both nails and staples of copper appeared nearly one thousand years earlier. Such nails were habitually used by Roman workmen. Archaeological excavations made in Scotland only a few years ago uncovered a store of about seven tons of copper nails, abandoned by the Romans sometime between A.D. 87 and 90.

A British Museum expedition worked at Tel el-Obeid, a mound near the site of ancient Ur in old Mesopotamia, under the direction of Sir Leonard Woolley. In 1924 they succeeded in clearing a small temple that had been buried in the mound. The reward was the discovery of artifacts of an entirely new type, completely unlike those found in nearby archaeological sites and executed in a technique previously quite unknown. The lavish use of copper was surprising.

Inside a porch, supported by columns, was an elaborate entrance, guarded on each side by the foreparts of two large copper lions. Above the door was a magnificent copper relief showing a large, double-headed eagle grasping the tails of two lifelike stags, standing back to back. On a ledge off the porch platform paraded a group a small copper bulls, all complete statuettes. The whole temple was banded by a series of friezes of copper lions and bulls. All these were made of copper plates, cemented to a wooden background with bitumen. The discovery of a foundation tablet there records that Aannipadda, king of Ur, built the temple, which is dated about 3100 B.C.

The mineral copper was named for the island of Cyprus, being a corruption of the name, for Cyprus means copper. From the beginning of mining there (ca. 4000 B.C.), Cyprus furnished copper from its rich mines to the ancient Mediterranean world. The Old Testament name "Isles of Chittim" refers to Cyprus and to the people who inhabited the island. Long before the iron hand of Rome held sway, copper ore and cast ingots were exported in vast quantities from the island. The American-operated Mavrovouni mine, near Lefka, once produced annually more than a million tons of raw copper from veins first mined about 3,000 years ago. The copper digs of Cyprus are still a valued resource.

Copper is frequently found in the pure, or native, form in nature, but rarely in great enough concentration to mine economically. The well-known exception is the Keweenaw Peninsula in upper Michigan with its great native copper deposits. Usually mining is dependent on one or more of the many copper compounds.

The primary ores used by the Hebrews were azurite, cuprite, and malachite, discovered by Dr. Nelson Glueck to be those mined in the famous copper mines of King Solomon, north of Ezion-geber and south of the Dead Sea. Copper mines have also been found in the Wadi Margharah (Valley of the Cave), in southwest Sinai, by Israelis.

The Gospel of Mark relates (speaking of Jesus), "And he sat down opposite the treasury, and watched the multitude putting money into the treasury. Many rich people put in large sums. And a poor widow came, and put in two copper coins, which make a penny" (Mark 12:41–42, R.S.V.). This shows that copper and the more precious metals were regularly coined in New Testament times.

John Scofield, senior editor of *National Geographic* magazine, made a fact-finding trip to Israel in 1952 and visited the ancient site of King Solomon's copper mines in the wind-scorched Wadi Araba. All that was to be seen was bare desert rock and a few pits scratched out by hopeful prospectors. A return trip in 1964 astounded him, for in the same spot he found all the structures of a huge copper-processing plant. Enormous pits now pockmarked the seared desert, and from them large earthmovers labored to hurry ore to the noisy crushers and concentrators. What a transformation!

The Western Hemisphere produces most of the copper so necessary for today's economy. Copper ranks second after iron as the most essential mineral in industry. In the United States, Arizona leads in the production of copper, although some other famous deposits are those at Bingham Canyon, Utah (a huge, open-pit mine); Butte, Montana; Ducktown, Tennessee (the largest copper mine in the eastern United States); and the Keweenaw Peninsula in northern Michigan on the shore of Lake Superior, where prehistoric Indians worked the deposits of native copper, so pure that "lake copper" is a standard of quality. Here the copper has been found in nodules from tiny flecks to an enormous boulder of 420 tons. The largest of all copper mines is located in Chile, at Chuquicamata, where there are reserves estimated at more than 850 million tons.

Copper, famous for the alloys composed of it and other metals, has achieved new status in a recent alloy in which it is combined with 3 percent or less of beryllium, achieving a metal of such strength that no sign of fatigue has been observed although a spring made from it has been vibrated 2 billion times! Other important alloys, known for many centuries, are brass (copper and zinc) and, most ancient of all, bronze (copper and tin).

See Brass; Bronze.

23. CORAL

Coral: the often branching, hornlike skeletons of various sea organisms; although an animal product, often resembles plantlike forms.

> But where shall wisdom be found?
> And where is the place of understanding?
> No mention shall be made of coral or of crystal;
> the price of wisdom is above pearls.
> Job 28:12, 18, R.S.V.

Even the sea contributes gems to man's storehouse of beauty. Coral, one of two peculiar gem materials furnished by the sea, the other being pearl, has an organic origin, being made of the skeletons of millions of minute marine animals. Not strictly mineral, its chemical composition is definitely allied to those of true gem materials. Associated with seaweeds and other ocean plants, corals are plantlike creatures. They present the appearance of a well-kept underwater garden as they grow in groups or fields. Living in colonies, individual citizens are tiny sea animals called polyps. Colonies extend as the polyps grow and multiply, taking food from seawater, as well as calcium carbonate, which is deposited in their tissues as crystalline calcite. New generations of polyps adhere to the accumulated growth of stonelike skeletons left from the calcite, repeating the life cycle again and again. Eventually the mass may become a dangerous reef or even be uplifted, forming an island.

Attaching itself by a disklike base to whatever hard substance nature provides, coral always grows at right angles from its base. If adhering to the bottom of a stone ledge, it will grow straight down; attached to the side, it will extend sideways. In this respect coral differs from a true plant, which always strives toward the sunlight. Living coral has an outer gelatinous area made of innumerable groups of polyps projecting like little warts all over the surface and surrounding the mineral-like skeleton. Coral flourishes within 90 feet of the water's surface, rarely growing below 150 feet in depth, where light is diminished, though it has been found as deep as 1,000 feet.

White coral occurs in huge quantities in warm seawaters, but the rare pink to deep-red species is found infrequently and is precious and highly desirable. Impurities in the mineral matter absorbed by the polyps give coral its attractive color shades. Most red gem coral is a branching type, bushlike in appearance, growing about a foot high with stems up to an inch in thickness. Expert polishing and carving of red coral makes it desirable for use in jewelry and small art objects.

Most coral used in Biblical times came from the Mediterranean Sea and the Persian Gulf. Today it is still gathered from Mediterranean waters. The most plentiful localities are the Algerian and Tunisian coasts, the western coasts of Sardinia and Corsica, and parts of the coast of Sicily. Coral is found sparsely in the western waters off Italy, and a few spots on the southern coasts of France and Spain also produce it. Oriental waters produce some red coral which usually ends up in the hands of the Chinese, who turn out exceptionally beautiful carved articles.

Coral must be harvested while still living. If the polyps die before a branch is brought to the surface, the coral turns dark, and its gem value is greatly decreased. On the shores of Sicily much dead coral continues to be brought up, caused perhaps by great quantities of volcanic ash thrown out by nearby volcanoes, muddying the waters and stifling the coral growth. Some red coral appears to be worm-eaten. In this condition it is regarded as worthless in Europe but is highly valued in India.

Precious coral was known and prized by many Near Eastern peoples, as well as by the Greeks and Romans. An ancient Assyrian text on glass-making indicates that workers making opaque, colored glass were concerned primarily with duplicating the distinctive colors of gem minerals. Red hues were an attempt to imitate coral rather than ruby.

During the Middle Ages precious coral was used as a medicinal astringent, a heart stimulant, a medicine for poisoning and fevers, and when powdered and mixed with pearls, a cure for colic and vomiting. Children wore it as a preventive against childhood ailments, and babies were believed protected in their sleep if a piece of coral was tied around their necks. When coral was worn in bunches as brooches, bracelets, or necklaces, people believed it made a charm to ward off evil spirits or bad luck.

Whereas red coral was formerly in great demand, now the rare black coral is highly prized. A spot in Hawaiian Island waters has furnished fine material. Recently, Luis Marden, of *National Geographic,* made the first known discovery of black coral in Jordanian waters in the Gulf of Aqaba. Some of this coral was cut into beads for a Moslem rosary, a *masbaha,* for King Hussein of Jordan.

Fossilized coral holds a great attraction for some mineral collectors. Petoskey stones, eagerly sought on the shore of Lake Michigan near Petoskey, are the remains of prehistoric coral. In Florida agate and chalcedony have replaced ancient coral, making a fossilized coral which is a decidedly different and beautiful cutting and polishing material for lapidaries.

24. CRYSTAL

Crystal: a solid body with a regular geometric form that denotes definite internal structure; to Bible peoples meant the clear quartz with its regular six sides and sharply pointed tip.

The gold and crystal cannot equal it; and the exchange of it shall not be for jewels of fine gold. Job 28:17, A.V.

> *Take in thy hand the Crystal bright,*
> *Translucent image of the Eternal Light;*
> *Pleased with its luster, every power divine*
> *Shall grant thy vows presented at their shrine;*
> *But how to prove the virtue of the stone,*
> *A certain mode to thee I will make known;*
> *To kindle without fire the sacred blaze,*
>
> . . . .
>
> *Yet though of flame the cause, strange to be told,*
> *The stone snatched from the blaze is icy cold.*

The lovely lines of this poem hint at attributes of the quartz crystal, particularly the ancient belief in its peculiar origin and its use as a lens to start a sacrificial fire. O. C. Farrington has modernized the poem to make it more significant and understandable. It is believed to have been written by Onomacritus, a Greek, about 510 B.C.

The origin of quartz crystals was the subject of strange beliefs. Ancient philosophers thought the hot, tropical sun ripened common stones into perfect crystals. Others believed the crystals to be permanently frozen water. Pliny said rock crystal originated from intense cold, and the idea that it was a form of ice prevailed until the beginning of the nineteenth century. Hebrew words, designating some clear, brilliant substance, can mean either "ice" or "crystal." Contrast the fourteenth century rendering of Psalm 147:17, "He sendis his kristall as morcels," with our modern version, "He casteth forth his ice like morsels" (A.V.).

Crystal has numerous Biblical references. The Authorized Version relates that St. John, describing the New Jerusalem, said, ". . . and her light was like unto a stone most precious, even like a jasper stone, clear as crystal" (Rev. 21:11). The Moffatt translation lists rock crystal as one of the covering stones of the Prince of Tyre (Ezek. 28:13), and crystal as the third stone in the first row of gems in the breastplate (Exod. 28:18). Although A. Paul Davis used rock crystal as a gem in his replica of the breastplate, he used it as an alternate for diamond.

Ancient cultures found many exotic uses for quartz crystals. Since faceting was then an unknown art, fine, small, natural crystals were often set or strung uncut. Some of the exquisitely formed quartz crystals from Herkimer County, New York, treated the same way, have made handsome jewelry. Quartz crystal lenses dated at about 3800 B.C. have been found in the ruins of Nineveh, but whether they were used for burning or magnifying, or even cauterizing wounds, is unknown. Other lenses discovered in Crete date from 1600 to 1200 B.C.

The Romans carved great blocks of crystal into enormous vases and bowls and fashioned goblets and drinking cups from smaller fragments. Evidently the hardened ice legend persisted during early Roman days, for quartz crystal cups were used for cold drinks and agate ones reserved for hot beverages.

Many ancient sources of quartz crystals are mentioned by Pliny and others. Listed are the Alps, Portugal, Cyprus, and Asia Minor, and contradicting the congealed ice theory, a Red Sea island, and India. Pliny recounts that rock crystal and citrine (yellow) quartz were dug from the same pits in Spain. The Egyptians were known to mine for quartz crystals and amethyst as early as 3500 B.C. near the present Aswan.

Quartz (silicon dioxide) is one of the most widely occurring minerals, and superb crystals are found in many localities, with Madagascar and Brazil producing them in enormous quantities. In the United States, the Hot Springs, Arkansas, area is famed for superior crystals. The quartz of Herkimer County, New York, noted for its exceptional crystal form and brilliance, is often referred to incorrectly as "Herkimer diamond." The Pikes Peak region of Colorado is well known to collectors for fine smoky quartz crystals dug from pegmatites during the past half-century.

Quartz crystals have become valuable in the industrial world because of several important characteristics. Quartz has a hardness of 7 on the mineral scale, harder than steel. It is quite tough under impact, since it does not cleave. It resists acids, being attacked only by hydrofluoric acid at an appreciable rate. A stable oxide itself, quartz cannot oxidize, and it withstands atmospheric weathering because it does not combine readily with water.

Long-distance telephone circuits use thin sections of quartz crystal cut and ground to respond to certain electrical frequencies. Several different sections make possible many conversations at the same time on the same line. Identical oscillator blanks unscramble the different voices at the other end, making them intelligible. Since the discovery in 1920 that the quartz crystal, used in radio sending sets, enables a large number of stations to operate simultaneously, each maintaining its own wave length or frequency exactly, quartz has been vital in this field of communication.

25. DIAMOND

Diamond: crystallized carbon; the hardest known substance; when transparent and without flaws, one of the most highly valued gemstones.

The sin of Judah is written with a pen of iron, and with the point of a diamond: it is graven upon the table of their heart, and upon the horns of your altars. Jeremiah 17:1, A.V.

Diamond—the flash of the betrothal symbol that decorates the third finger of a girl's left hand.

Diamond—the almost invisible sliver that produces majestic music on a phonograph.

Diamond—the extremely hard point that enables a drill to cut through rock.

In 1967, the United States imported about 3½ tons, or more than 15,763,000 carats,* of diamonds for American industry, and more than 3,961,000 carats for jewels. Modern use contrasts sharply with Old Testament times. Nothing indicates that the diamond was used or even known then, and considerable doubt exists that the gemstone was familiar to early New Testament people. Among the treasures of ancient rulers, turquoise, lapis lazuli, and rock crystal were far more likely to be found than emeralds, sapphires, and rubies. Diamonds, never!

Theophrastus (372–287 B.C.) does not include the stone in his listing of gems, but Pliny describes the new bipyramidal diamond crystals from India about A.D. 77. However, they were extremely rare. Marco Polo, on his return from Cathay (China) in the thirteenth century, was the first to bring any number of diamonds to Western civilization.

"The sin of Judah is written with a pen of iron, and with the point of a diamond . . ." (Jer. 17:1) is the only significant mention of diamond in the Authorized Version. Knowing the facts, one finds it hard to believe that diamond was actually the stone meant. Those who maintain that diamond and adamant were the same lack sufficient proof. Originally, Biblical adamant seems to have been a hard metal rather than a stone as implied much later. But if the point of the stylus actually was diamond, its use, even then, would have been industrial!

Diamond was named, also, as the third stone of the second row of gems set in the breastplate of the high priest. "And the third row shall be an emerald, a sapphire, and a diamond" (Exod. 28:18. A.V.). The frontispiece to this book which illustrates the breastplate shows a beautiful gem of rock crystal, which A. Paul Davis believes was the gemstone used.

Preeminent in the realm of gems, the diamond has been highly regarded by many peoples. In some parts of the world, "diamond fever" has been as virulent as "gold fever" in the United States. Two Greek words meaning "that which cannot be broken" or "unconquerable"

---

* The measured weight of gems, the carat, said to equal four drops of water or the weight of a dry seed of the carab tree, was standardized in 1907. One carat is 200 milligrams, or ⅕ gram. The carat is divided into 100 points for greater accuracy.

(because of the stone's hardness) gave the diamond its name, and it has become a symbol of power and fearlessness. A mistaken belief maintained that the gem could not be shattered. The story is told that the earliest test for a diamond's hardness was to place the crystal on an anvil and strike it with a heavy hammer. If it remained unbroken, it passed the test! Considering the highly perfect cleavage of the diamond crystal, one shudders to think of the number of genuine, flawless diamonds destroyed by this ignorant treatment.

The earliest known diamonds came from India, and until the beginning of the eighteenth century, India was the best if not the only source. Many famous diamonds are Indian, including the celebrated Kohinoor (now in the British crown jewels) and the blue Hope diamond (in the Smithsonian Institution). During Africa's ascent in the production of diamonds, some famous ones were discovered. The original Star of Africa (the Cullinan rough), the largest diamond known to man (discovered in 1905), weighed 1⅓ pounds, 3,106 carats. From it were cut nine large stones, including the Cullinan I (530.20 carats) and Cullinan II (317.40 carats) and numerous smaller gems. In 1967 the world's seventh-largest diamond of 601.25 carats was found in South Africa. The golf-ball-sized stone was named the Lesotho diamond. Harry Winston, New York diamond dealer, is reputed to have paid $600,000 for it.

The origin of the diamond is still unsolved. One certain fact is known: the primary diamond deposits are in diamond pipes. These pipes are funnel-like, somewhat oval in shape and narrowing with depth. The full depth is unknown, although some have been mined at more than 4,000 feet. They are of volcanic origin and are filled with material called kimberlite or blue ground. It is named after Kimberley, South Africa, location of the famed Kimberley mine, so extensively dug that it is now the world's largest man-made crater, 1,520 feet across and 3,601 feet deep. It is in the kimberlite that diamonds occur. The diamond is usually found as an eight-sided (octahedral) crystal, although it also occurs in other crystal shapes, and is usually colorless or nearly so. The colored diamonds (the fancies), rarest of all precious stones, such as the blue Hope diamond, the canary-yellow Tiffany, and the Dresden green, are all world renowned.

Diamonds, acid-resistant and supremely hard, are of incalculable value in industry. A tool made of the hardest and toughest of man-made products, tungsten carbide, can incise a groove 21 miles long in bronze before sharpening is needed, but a diamond cuts 1,200 miles! A drilled diamond for drawing wire will make up to 15,000 miles of copper wire before requiring a redrilling.

In Murfreesboro, Arkansas, typical blue ground and some diamonds are found. Would-be prospectors may hunt for diamonds by paying a modest fee. Occasionally a real find is made; in 1956 a housewife located a 15½-carat rough diamond, the Star of Arkansas.

26. EMERALD

Emerald: a variety of beryl, highly prized as a gemstone because of its unrivaled rich green color; one of the rarest of gems.

And he that sat was to look upon like a jasper and a sardine stone: and there was a rainbow round about the throne, in sight like unto an emerald. *Revelation 4:3,* A.V.

Cases of mistaken identity can be distressing, tragic, amusing, or confusing. As for the emerald, the latter situation certainly applies. Exodus 39, describing the making of the high priest's breastplate, says, "And they set in it four rows of stones: the first row was a sardius, a topaz, and a carbuncle. . . . And the second row, an emerald, a sapphire, and a diamond" (Exod. 39:10–11, A.V.). In Hebrew, *nōphĕk,* meaning a shining stone, applied to the carbuncle; *bāreqeth,* meaning glittering, described the emerald. For no known reason the King James translators reversed the terms, thus changing the order of the precious stones in the breastplate. So we have confusion!

The depth of green of the emerald's beauty caused various ancient cultures to use the stone as a symbol of spring and the earth's guardian of generation and ripening. It was believed to strengthen memory and eloquence, to foster prevision, and to be a warrant for honesty and reliability in early eras. Since it was supposed to measure a lover's fervor, it was the favorite stone of Venus. In Mohammedan belief, emerald is the first heaven. Symbolic significance was attached to different gems. Emerald, its green likened to the cool verdure of earth, meant tranquillity. History records that Julius Caesar fancied emeralds because he believed they had potent curative powers.

The emerald mines of Upper Egypt became famous in Cleopatra's time. The glamorous queen often wore the gems to enhance her beauty and frequently gave emeralds as gifts to those she wished particularly favored. These mines were located near Zabara, not far from the Red Sea, at the southern border of Egypt. Alexander the Great may have mined these deposits originally. After Cleopatra's time the mines were abandoned and forgotten. Ages passed, and the workings were at last rediscovered, with mining tools at hand, just as they had been left centuries before by miners searching for the precious green stone. Emeralds found in the ruins of Pompeii and Herculaneum probably came from the mines in Upper Eygpt.

The glamor stone of the beautiful beryl family of minerals is the emerald. Of velvety, intensely deep green, it may be the rarest of gems, as well as the most valuable. Its unsurpassed color, produced by minute amounts of chromium oxide, is its distinguishing mark. Although a little softer than some gems, but still as hard as or harder than quartz, this is of no consequence considering the beauty of the stone. Emerald is more easily fractured than other varieties of beryl. The characteristic steplike pattern of faceting has given the name "emerald cut" to this style of cutting. Only rarely some emeralds are cut in the "brilliant" style of the diamond. Ancient stones were always cut in the rounded, or *cabochon*, form.

The old saying, "An emerald without a flaw," denotes nearly unattainable perfection, for a flawless emerald is almost unknown. Emerald is considerably marred by internal fractures and by cloudy and discolored areas. The inferior index of refraction of emerald is the basis of its lack of brilliance compared to diamond. Emerald is the apex of the beryl family. No other member even approaches it in vivid hue, depth of coloring, clarity, and rarity.

Although worked intermittently, the mines in Colombia, South America, at Muzo, Chivor, and Coscuez have furnished most of the emerald crystals of the world for several years. Colombia was the source of the fantastic collection of emeralds, many intricately and beautifully carved, of the ancient Inca civilization.

The Incas guarded some of their emeralds in sacred temples where they worshiped them. Rather than have their loved gems fall into the hands of the Spanish conquistadors, Inca priests told the conquerors that true emeralds could not be broken, and so deliberately caused many beautiful stones to be shattered as the conquerors attempted to prove they were genuine. The Incas purposely camouflaged their mines from the white men. While some mines were rediscovered by accident, many may still remain hidden. The size and color of the gems brought from the New World far outshone the stones previously known or acquired by the Spanish, including those brought to Western Europe from the Orient by the Crusaders and Marco Polo.

An American, Willis F. Bronkie, supervises the operation of the world's largest privately owned emerald mine, the famed Chivor mine in Colombia. One of the ancient Inca mines, the Chivor was not successfully hidden from the Spanish, who mined the lode, using Indian slave labor, for more than a hundred years. Abandoned in the last quarter of the seventeenth century, it was rediscovered in 1896 by the use of old Spanish records for directions. Today the Chivor mine produces about one-third of the world's supply of emeralds.

Many countries produce emeralds. Some of the important areas are in Brazil, Australia, Austria, Norway, South Africa, the Ural Mountains of the U.S.S.R., and in the United States, North Carolina. Egypt remains a producing source of the ancient gem, emerald.

27. FLINT

Flint: a massive, dark-colored, microcrystalline variety of quartz hard enough to strike fire with steel.

Who led thee through that great and terrible wilderness, wherein were fiery serpents, and scorpions, and drought, where there was no water; who brought thee forth water out of the rock of flint. . . . *Deuteronomy 8:15,* R.V.

Flint! What a variety of choices when one considers this subject! The name is given to tiny objects chipped to sharp points or to sharp cutting edges, such as arrowheads, used by primitive man for hunting, and scrapers to clean the animal skins when the hunt was over. It could be a larger rock to strike fire with steel. A chipped piece of flint secured in the hammer of a seventeenth-century gun produced a flash of fire when it forcibly hit the iron cover of the powder pan to fire the charge of loose powder. We are most concerned with flint as a mineral and its mineralogical qualities.

Flint is a cryptocrystalline variety of quartz and is a very hard, sometimes brittle, rock. Flint is similar to chalcedony but more opaque and of dull, dark colors, usually smoky gray, smoky brown, or brownish black. It breaks with a very decided conchoidal (shell-like) fracture, leaving an extremely sharp cutting edge. Numerous other varieties of quartz, when used by primitive man in the making of tools and weapons, are often confused with flint. Because of their use in this way, many quartz mineral artifacts are called flints, relating not to the material, but to the fact they were utilized as implements by man in prehistoric times. Such flints, including axes, celts (chisels), scrapers, knives, arrowheads, and spear points, are an exceedingly important record of the story of early man.

The creation of flint is a lengthy chemical reaction. Fresh water is known for its ability to dissolve most minerals, and the predominantly silica portion of flint, originally part of the rock from which the crust of our earth is made, is broken up by erosion and dissolved by water. Silica in solution (colloidal silica) is carried by freshwater streams to the ocean. This is the second most abundant soluable substance added to seawaters annually, and amounts to nearly 12 percent of these materials. Salt water, however, cannot maintain a mineral in solution for any length of time, so the major part of the silica is precipitated. If considerable clay is deposited, the silica becomes part of it. (Silica is a partial component of the adhesiveness of clay.) The clay is the origin of the common shale we are familiar with. Later these clay muds were covered by depositions of other materials.

If the river waters are clear and carry only materials in solution, the silica brought into the ocean collects until it reaches the saturation point. Then the salts in the seawater cause its precipitation usually in the form of a jelly-like mass containing water. If these harden before deposition of other sediments cover them, they retain their shape as nodules. If subjected to pressure by the heavy deposits of calcium carbonate (calcite) or magnesium carbonate (dolomite), the silica mass is flattened and becomes a lens. If the calcite, which settles to the sea floor as an extremely fine mud, becomes rock that is porous and soft, it is chalk. Because of additional pressure and consolidation it becomes firm and hard limestone. In the buckling and shifting of the earth's crust, exposed ocean floors of great age show large deposits of chalk and limestone, and in them many concretions of flint, as well as chert, coated white from their contact with the host deposits. Such are the chalk cliffs of Dover, containing nodules of black flint.

Flint is quite common in Palestine, and many Bible passages mention it. The Book of Deuteronomy relates that it was from a rock of flint that water flowed for the Children of Israel in the desert. Another reference uses the phrase "oil out of the flinty rock" (Deut. 32:13), indicating that olive groves grew on flinty soil. Interestingly, for a long period of time no one comprehended how olive trees could possibly grow in the location and soil of the Negeb. There were no pools of underground waters or springs to provide needed moisture for the trees. Then a great many stone walls, built in the form of small circles, were found in the Negeb. Inside each circular wall, when the sand was removed, were found the roots of an olive tree which had grown centuries ago. The loosely stacked stones of the walls allowed the wind to blow through them, carrying airborne moisture. As temperatures dropped during the night, dew collected on the inside surface of the walls, providing sufficient moisture for a single tree (or sometimes a single grapevine) to grow.

In Joshua 5, the leader of the Israelites is commanded to make knives of flint to circumcize his people. Joshua made sharp knives and carried out the command (5:2). It seemed this rite had been neglected during the later years of their slavery in Egypt, the neglect continuing through the wilderness wanderings. It is evident that the Lord desired circumcision as a final act of dissociation from the degrading and spiritless life led by Israelites under slavery in Egypt.

The earliest known knives were of flint or some similar stone. A beautifully formed Egyptian flint knife from Jebel el Arak and believed to be of the proto-dynastic epoch is described by Georges Contenau, honorary chief curator of the Louvre. Though the blade is flint, the handle is of ivory carved with a great many small figures of animals of many species and numerous human figures and had once been covered with burnished gold leaf.

Flint knives continued in use for centuries, maintaining their traditional place in certain religious ceremonies. Knives and other implements have been found throughout the world, scattered wherever primitive civilizations became established, and changes to metal tools indicate the progress of these people.

28. GLASS

Glass: a noncrystalline, amorphous substance, usually transparent, made by the fusing, under intense heat, of three common minerals or materials of mineral origin: sand, soda, and lime.

And the building of the wall of it was of jasper: and the city was pure gold, like unto clear glass. *Revelation 21:18, A.V.*

"And before the throne there was a sea of glass like unto crystal . . ." (Rev. 4:6). Technically, glass is not a mineral and cannot be classified as such. Yet one can stretch a point in the listing of Biblical minerals because glass is the result of fusing three common substances man has utilized for centuries: sand, soda, and lime. The sand was composed mostly of tiny quartz grains; the soda was natron, from the natural saline lakes in many areas; and the lime was actually calcite, obtained from the plentiful limestone deposits. Glass "like unto crystal" (transparent) suggests that such glass was distinctly unusual; most glass of earliest antiquity was opaque and colored.

When or how the making of glass was discovered is unknown. Pliny recounted that Phoenician sailors anchored their vessel and built a fire on the white sands of the beach. Part of their cargo was natron, a natural sodium carbonate. Lumps of this might have supported their kettles. How amazed they must have been to see glass form under the fire's heat from the reaction of the soda of the natron, the potash from the wood ashes, and fine beach sand!

An interesting tale, but the art of glassmaking was probably discovered even earlier by Egyptian priests. Glass relics from Egyptian tombs date back to 3500 B.C., but regular production of glass in Egypt did not begin until the early part of the eighteenth dynasty (1580–1350 B.C.). During this period glassmaking reached a high degree of perfection. Skillful imitations of gemstones, made of colored glass pastes, were valued as highly as the gems themselves.

Archaeological finds have revealed evidence of the great antiquity of glass and the extraordinary proficiency of glassworkers. A cuneiform tablet unearthed at Nineveh, when translated, was found to be a seventeenth-century B.C. text on glassmaking. Assyrian glassmaking began with the usual alkali-lime-sand combination. Sand furnished silica, calcium carbonate from natural limestone deposits furnished the lime, and the leaching of salt-marsh grasses provided soda. Using the formulas, Assyrian glassworkers turned out surprisingly large batches of nearly colorless, high-alkali glass as a kind of raw material. By melting a definite weight of this powdered base material with metallic oxides, they secured colored glasses of many hues.

In coloring glass, great emphasis was placed on blues and reds. Blue glass of several different shades usually had a copper origin On rare occasions, the typical dark-blue glass simulating lapis lazuli was colored by a small amount of cobalt. Red glass (to have the appearance of red jasper) owed its color to the copper compound cuprite rather than to gold as in modern ruby glass. This was proven when a fragment of badly deteriorated red glass with a coating of green on its surface was found. The coating met the distinctive test for copper. Gold was used in one type of glass to secure a coral-red color, imitating the beautiful red coral found in the Persian Gulf. Chemical analysis has shown tin in most white opaque glass. Antimony oxide provided two quite different effects in glass, according to the amount of heat used. One heat produced brilliantly clear, colorless glass objects; another put color in the glass melt or turned it opaque. Some yellow glass had lead and antimony as unusual coloring agents. Green was probably secured by iron, as is the case with some modern glass.

Glassmakers of ancient cultures did not understand chemistry, so the making of glass was a matter of trial and error. The ingredients were far from pure, resulting in variations in color, texture, and quality. Though the causes of an effect might be unknown, the ancient workers understood what results could be obtained from certain mineral materials. Though ancient glass was molded and shaped by rods and sticks, almost none was blown. Blown glass appeared first in Roman times, during an era beginning about 30 B.C.

Modern civilization prides itself on efficient distribution, but ancient tradesmen evolved similar methods centuries ago. Wide dispersal of identical types of glass prove there were distant-ranging trade routes 2,000 years ago, from the Mediterranean coasts to the heart of Asia. Dealers a thousand miles apart could order glassware from the same glassmaker and have it safely delivered by caravan. Glassworkers even ordered special ingredients or rough glass blocks from a wholesale jobber. One bit of proof is that two pieces of known Roman glass of the same general composition have been found 2,000 miles apart.

Modern man has succeeded in casting two enormous blanks weighing twenty tons each for use as lenses in the Hale Telescope. However, a recent archaeological expedition revealed the third-largest casting of glass in the world. The huge slab of opaque, raspberry-colored glass weighs nearly nine tons. It is 11 feet long, 6½ feet wide, and 1½ feet thick. Discovered in a cave at Beth She'arim, where the Israelis planned to make a museum, its purpose is totally unknown. Modern scientists are amazed at the technological achievements of 1,400 years ago that allowed the casting of this enormous piece of glass, made where it was found and where legend says mankind discovered how to make glass.

29. GOLD

Gold: a bright yellow metallic element, the most precious of all metals, the most easily shaped or drawn of all metals, and one of the heaviest.

Surely there is a vein for the silver, and a place for gold where they fine it. Job 28:1, A.V.

If a person had six names one might suspect him of being of royal descent. Gold certainly qualifies in this respect! It is truly a royal mineral, the leader of all others. In the Hebrew, it actually had at least six names: *sᵉgōr*, carefully preserved; *kĕthĕm*, the preserved thing; *päz*, purified; *bĕṣĕr*, broken off; *chārūtz*, dug out; and *zähäb*. The word *zähäb* had several qualifying prefixed terms referring to characteristics and the many attributes of gold.

Gold is the most famous of earth's elements. Though widely distributed, sizable concentrations are rare. Occurring in nature in the "native" state, it was probably the first metal known to man. Pure gold has a characteristic yellow color which does not tarnish and goes through fire without color change caused by oxidation.

Since man's earliest contact with gold many interesting facts have been learned. Gold usually occurs in threads from fine to thick, as scales, grains, and occasionally in masses called nuggets. When it is found in its original location, one of the two general ways it occurs, it is said to be *in situ*. In this case it is usually found in quartz veins, though it does occur in several types of rocks. When the matrix in which gold occurs weathers away, the gold frequently washes into stream beds, to be concentrated in sands or gravels, even in sea beaches. This is called placer gold (the second main type) and is usually mined by washing, a process known as placer mining.

Placer gold from alluvial deposits was the first and usual source for the gold seeker. Egyptian monuments of the first dynasty, around 2900 B.C., depict the washing of gold ore. From classical mythology comes the legend of Jason and his Argonauts who set sail in their ship Argo (*ca.* 1200 B.C.) in search of the Golden Fleece. This famous adventure had as its goal the seizure of the extremely fine gold dust caught in sheepskins by the mining inhabitants of Colchis (later known as Armenia).

Placer gold is found from fine dust to large nuggets. A nugget of 161 pounds was found in California, but even larger ones have been found in Australia. One famous nugget, the Welcome Stranger Nugget, weighed more than 190 pounds, but the largest found in the Australian gold rush days of 1851 was the Holtermann Nugget, weighing more than 200 pounds.

The leading gold-producing mine in the United States is the Homestake Mine at Lead, South Dakota, a lode mine. It produces about 600,000 ounces of gold each year and has been a producing mine for almost a century. Since 1877, the Homestake has produced 27,333,000 ounces of gold. Figured at $35 per ounce, this would be $956,655,000. The richest gold region is the Rand area in South Africa, where the deepest mines are located. The district around Johannesburg has yielded more than $12 billion since the discovery of gold there in 1886. Some of the air-conditioned mines are more than 9,000 feet deep.

Gold is the most malleable of all metals. A bit of gold smaller than the size of a pinhead, weighing one grain, can be beaten into gold leaf only 1/250,000 of an inch thick which covers an area of 56 square inches. Gold is also an extremely ductile metal. The same amount of gold can be drawn into a wire nearly 500 feet long.

Palestine had no known sources of gold, but the Hebrews were familiar with mining operations from observing the Egyptians in their ventures in Sinai. Biblical descriptions of mining attest to this fact. Gold was imported from foreign sources: the land of Havilah, the sand land (possibly near Damascus); Parvaim Uphaz; Tarshish (the high country); and perhaps from Egypt, Midian, Sheba (Arabia), Africa, and Ophir (believed to be on the west coast of India, though the location is uncertain).

In early days Arabia was mentioned as the source of much gold which was brought to Tyre from Sheba and Rama by Arabian merchants. The questionable Tarshish might be identified as an area in Spain. In the first book of the Maccabees, gold and silver mines are mentioned: "Now Judas heard of the fame of the Romans . . . and what they had done in the country of Spain, for the winning of the mines of silver and gold which is there" (I Macc. 8:1, 3).

The art of working gold is of great antiquity. Most ancient peoples were skilled in mining, smelting, refining, and fabricating the metal. In the royal tombs of Ur, excavated by Sir Leonard Woolley, fabulous items of jewelry and personal adornment were found. An exquisite crown of delicately wrought leaves, garters of gold and lapis lazuli, and dainty cosmetic boxes were uncovered. One box is shaped like a fragile golden shell, while a paint cup with an intricate inlay of lapis lazuli and carnelian has an edging of tiny ostrich eggs of gold. Only the golden tomb of Tutankhamen equals the fabulous collection of golden artifacts found at Ur, with the Sumer tombs preceding the Egyptian one by about a thousand years.

The Israelites learned how to treat gold early in their history. Some of the oldest writings contain allusions to the goldsmith's art. Familiar with the efficient Egyptian procedures of smelting gold, Old Testament writers mention the working of the bellows and the use of lead in refining. The ore was hand-sorted, crushed, powdered, and concentrated by washing. The crude concentrate was melted with lead, and this alloy then combined with more lead and salt. Draft for the furnaces was furnished by a pair of bellows which the operator alternately pulled up with cords and compressed with his feet. Four or five days of this treatment removed most of the impurities, which passed off in slag. Remelted, the gold was of high purity.

Though Solomon and others imported gold and silver from many sources, the art of working them was introduced from Phoenicia. The goldsmith was often referred to as the "refiner," who knew how to remove impurities from the metal by melting it in the "refining pot" and then fashioning it into ornamental or useful articles.

Numerous methods of working the precious metal were practiced: beating or hammering (Exod. 25:18); plating or overlaying (Exod. 25:11; I Kings 6:20); and soldering (Isa. 41:7). Casting, pouring melted metal into a shaped mold, is implied by the "molten image" (Num. 33:52). A clear distinction seems to have been made between the "graven image" and the "molten image" (Nah. 1:14; II Chron. 34:3–4).

Gold and its sister mineral, silver, were refined by melting, separating the dross from the pure metal and hastening it by adding an alkali flux. Many utensils of the goldsmith—hammer, tongs, chisel, anvil, graving tools, crucible, bellows, and melting oven—are mentioned in the Scriptures.

Like other nations of that time, the Hebrews esteemed gold highly. Solomon acquired enormous amounts of gold for decorating the Temple through his naval expeditions. Contributions of gold for the Temple were made by the Queen of Sheba and Hiram of Tyre. David, at his death, left to Solomon a tremendous supply of the precious metal, amassed as spoils of war. The Old Testament account (I Chron. 18:10–11) relates that David brought gold from Edom, Ammon, Philistia, and other victorious campaigns which he dedicated "unto the Lord." Tremendous amounts of gold changed hands as a result of military defeats and the levying of tribute and ransom.

Solomon dispatched a number of ships, manned by his servants and experienced sailors lent by King Hiram of Tyre, from Ezion-geber at the head of the Gulf of Aqaba. Their destination was Ophir. Returning from the lengthy voyage, they delivered 420 talents of gold to Solomon. Since the ancient Hebrew talent of gold had an estimated value of more than $32,000, this cargo was worth well in excess of $13 million (I Kings 9:26–28, A.V.).

Gold was plentiful in the reigns of David and Solomon, and it was used lavishly. In the Tabernacle, the ark cherubims, tables, candlesticks, altar, and many vessels were made of it. The Temple and king's palace were overlaid or gilded with the precious metal—even the walls, doors, floors, and roof.

Methods of soldering were used, and references indicate that Hebrew workmen were proficient in smoothing and polishing gold. They knew how to plate; though the exact manner is unknown, it might have been "overlay" in earliest eras. In the second millennium B.C. many objects were covered with thin sheets of gold. The sheets, or leaf, were made much as they are today. Gold was cast in small blocks, then rolled into thin plates. These were placed between skins and beaten with stone hammers. Gold sheets were cemented to wooden surfaces with gesso, a whitish plaster with some type of glue added. With its hard surface, gesso would permit the gold to be burnished. Even some bronze vessels were gilded, the thin gold surface put on with an adhesive gum.

Coinage was unknown to the Hebrews until after the Exile, though gold was used as a medium of exchange in the time of Abraham (ca.

2000 B.C.) by weight. Then wedges, bars, rings, and round flat disks were used. Even ear and finger rings were used as money. Bars or ingot circulated as money generally conformed to a standard, though ordinarily the bars were not weighed unless large or precise amounts were involved. Coinage really began in Palestine about the time of Ezra (536 B.C.).

Many examples of the handiwork of ancient goldsmiths which have been found illustrate their knowledge of gold's malleable and ductile qualities. One artifact of hammered gold is believed to have been made as early as 3500 B.C. Exquisite examples of drawn and hammered gold jewelry made millenniums before Christ are housed in museums throughout the world. Small threads, cut from extremely thin gold sheets, were woven into rare and costly cloth (Exod. 28:6). This was likely the thread with which Aaron's vestments were embroidered. "They did beat the gold into thin plates, and cut it into wire, to work it into the blue, and in the purple, and in the scarlet, and in the fine linen, with cunning work" (Exod. 39:3, A.V.).

30. HYACINTH

Hyacinth: a variety of zircon, transparent, brown to reddish-orange in color; suitable for use as a gemstone, although ancient cultures used the name "hyacinth" for a blue gem.

You are to make the pectoral of judgment. . . . In this you are to set four rows of stones . . . the third, hyacinth, ruby, amethyst. *Exodus 28:15, 17, 19, J.B.*

It is astonishing how many diverse meanings one word can acquire. The word "hyacinth" is no exception. One is a plant, fabled in classic myth, that sprang from the blood of Hyacinthus, a beautiful Greek youth— friend of the god Apollo, who caused the lovely blue-violet flower to grow when the lad met his death in a game of quoits. It might be the fragrant, spring-flowering bulb plant we all know. A third meaning is a color, bluish-purple in hue. Further, it is a precious blue stone of the ancients, so defined by Webster. More recently, it is authoritatively given as the name for a transparent red to brown variety of zircon, sometimes used as a gem.

To describe the gem "hyacinth" will require two descriptions. One is of the modern hyacinth. Today's usage of the name says it is a variety of zircon, as are the gems with the unusual names jacinth, jargon (jargoon), and ligure, jacinth often being used synonymously for hyacinth. Hyacinth is a somewhat uncommon mineral, usually found with other zircons in the gem gravels of Ceylon, the isle of gems. At Mudgee, New South Wales, fine hyacinths have been found as pebbles. Zircons of many colors, with a hardness of 7.5 and high refractive index, are lovely gems.

Ancient peoples used zircon as a medium for carving and engraving, but they probably did not call it hyacinth, though "ligure" may have been used to identify it. Since the gem cracked easily in working, most engravings show shallowness of figure and roundness of line, used by the ancient artists to prevent ruining the gem.

The second hyacinth is that of the people of ancient times. It has been defined as a blue stone in the beginning paragraph. *The Jerusalem Bible* uses hyacinth to indicate a hue of blue in St. John's vision in Revelation: "In my vision I saw the horses, and the riders with their breastplates of flame colour, hyacinth-blue and sulphur yellow" (9:17). Jacinth is still used as a synonym, for the Moffatt translation renders the same verse: ". . . they wore coats of mail red as fire, dark blue as jacinth, and yellow as smoke." The verse is also translated to indicate the gemstone which automatically brings to mind a blue gem—the sapphire.

After reading these translations of the same verse there can be little doubt that hyacinth, jacinth, and sapphire all refer to a blue gemstone. The true sapphire as we know it may have been the blue gem named in the New Testament, perhaps in the above passage. However, in Old Testment times, we believe the sapphire was not yet known, the use of corundum (of which sapphire is a variety) likely being limited to a small fragment or chip for incising or engraving softer stones.

The Greek *huakinthos* or Latin *hyacinthus*, translated as "hyacinth" or "jacinth" in several translations, seems to have been sapphire by New Testament times. The classical *hyacinthus* was blue, and the Septuagint used *huakinthos* for the Hebrew *t^ekēlĕth* as the descriptive word for the Tabernacle furnishings wherever "blue" is now used and meant in English. The Hebrew word *săppîr* of the Old Testament, often translated "sapphire," seems to have been lapis lazuli, a beautiful blue opaque gem.

In Revelation, two different blue gemstones are named as foundation stones, sapphire and jacinth, or two other blue stones, turquoise or lapis lazuli (21:19–20).

See Jacinth; Ligure; Zircon; Lapis Lazuli; Sapphire.

31. IRON

Iron: a gray metallic element, both malleable and ductile, strongly attracted by magnets; rare in pure form in nature, usually found combined with other elements.

. . . the Eternal your God is bringing you into a fine country, . . . where you shall lack for nothing, a country whose ore is iron and from whose hills you can dig copper. *Deuteronomy 8:7, 9, Moffatt.*

An entirely new metal, valued more highly than silver or gold, appeared in the seaports of Canaan about 1200 B.C. The Egyptians had known about it for 2,000 years, but it was extremely rare and unusual. It was iron! The Egyptians knew nothing of iron deposits in the earth. They possessed only the meteoric metal that plunged flaming from the skies. "Daggers from heaven" was the name given to the few weapons manufactured from this material.

The monopoly of iron held by the Hittites, a people living north of the Holy Land between the Black Sea and the Mediterranean, seems to have been broken at about this time in history. Although the Israelites did not use the metal, the Canaanites, living on the plains along the Mediterranean and into the hills to the east, are believed to have been using iron before the coming of the Philistines.

Following the death of Joshua, the sons of Judah, allied with the tribe of Simon, began the conquest of Canaan. They attacked the Canaanites who lived in the highlands, the Negeb, and the lowlands. Judah failed to overcome some of the Canaanites. "The Lord was with Judah, so that he conquered the highlands, although he was not able to conquer the inhabitants of the plain, because they had iron chariots" (Judges 1:19, S.-G.).

Before 1200 B.C., a horde of invaders known as the Peoples of the Sea swept in from the Aegean, capturing Crete, ravaging the Hittite country, and advancing along the eastern Mediterranean coast. Nothing stayed their progress. One after another great fortified cities, then whole nations, fell before them. They looted the famous silver mines of Tarsus and seized as plunder the swift chariot horses of Cilicia. Their greatest prize was the secret of the smelting and manufacture of iron, once the valuable monopoly of the Hittite kingdom.

The invaders pressed to the south until an aroused and fearful Egypt raised a huge army to oppose them. Under Rameses III, the Egyptians inflicted a stunning defeat upon the foreign hordes. There were still the invading ships, which had penetrated the mouth of the Nile, to deal with. Again the Egyptians achieved a decisive victory. This was 1188 B.C. Defeated, the foreigners preempted the coastal plain of southern Canaan, becoming the Philistines of the Old Testament. One great factor of their strength was their well-guarded secret of smelting iron. By refusing to give the Israelites any knowledge of working with iron, the Philistines were able to have many military successes over their enemy and to acquire many lands of the Israelites. While under the domination of the Philistines, the Israelites were not permitted to practice blacksmithing. "There was not a single smith in the whole land of Israel, because the Philistines had reasoned: We must prevent the Hebrews from forging swords or spears" (I Sam. 13:19, J.B.). When only Saul and Jonathan of the whole Israelite army had swords or spears on the day of the battle of Michmash, it must be assumed that iron swords were meant, being superior to those of copper or even bronze.

The Philistine hold on ironworking began to weaken with David's conquests, and at last he overcame the Philistines, winning for Israel the secret of making iron.

Iron now came into general use in Israel, and it was amassed for the building of the Temple. "And David prepared iron in abundance for the nails for the doors of the gates, and for the joinings" (I Chron. 22:3, A.V.). Archaeology substantiates that iron had been withheld from the Israelites, becoming their property only when the Philistines were conquered. Excavations have revealed numerous iron relics of 1100 B.C. and earlier in Philistia, but none predate 1100 B.C. in the hill country of Palestine where the Israelites lived.

Sir Flinders Petrie and Lady Hilda Petrie discovered the ruins of the ancient Philistine city Gerar, where four iron furnaces and a sword factory were found, and located nearby iron weapons including spearheads, daggers, chisels, and other implements made of iron.

Job says, "Canst thou draw out leviathan with a hook? . . . Canst thou fill his skin with barbed irons, or his head with fish spears?" (41:1, 7, A.V.), suggestions that iron spears and fishhooks were in use at this time. Also mentioned is the iron stylus, an ancient writing instrument (19:24).

Before recent discoveries, it was believed that Israel's iron came from foreign areas. Exploration by Dr. Nelson Glueck revealed that the Wadi Arabah, stretching south to the Gulf of Aqabah, on the Red Sea, once teemed with primitive towns where mining and smelting of iron as well as copper was carried on during the Iron Age.

After the Hebrews were fully established in Canaan, the occupation of smith or metalworker became a distinctive employment. These crafts are mentioned in many Biblical passages. Preparing iron for use in war, agriculture, or other domestic needs was one of the earliest applications of skilled labor. Smiths also worked in copper and bronze.

About 600 years before Christ, iron was one of the most important items of trade in Tyre's flourishing market. The Smith-Goodspeed translation tells of the "wrought iron" procured there (Ezek. 27:14). From this imported material, Hebrew blacksmiths made many objects to improve living standards—adzes, saws, pots, nails, plows, etc.

In Ecclesiasticus 38:28 (Smith-Goodspeed), one finds a vivid picture of the blacksmith at work:

> It is so with the smith sitting by his anvil,
> And expert in working in iron;
> The smoke of the fire reduces his flesh,
> And he exerts himself in the heat of the furnace.
> He bends his ear to the sound of the hammer,
> And his eyes are on the pattern of the implement,
> He puts his mind on completing his work,
> And he is anxious to finish preparing it.

After the capture of Jerusalem, King Nebuchadnezzar took the blacksmiths of Israel and other craftsmen as captives to Babylon.

Drab as life was, the Hebrews loved color and used it lavishly. Here they made unwitting use of iron, for iron compounds furnished several of the wanted colors. Red coloring was secured from red ocher, or powdered hematite, an iron oxide which is a soft, deep red. Yellows came from yellow ocher, another iron oxide, differing from the red in that there is considerably more water in its composition.

Other uses of iron compounds have come to light through archaeology. Hematite was used in carved forms by ancient man just as it is by modern man. Large polished surfaces of hematite make excellent mirrors, as do iron pyrites, the iron sulfide. Large numbers of iron pyrite mirrors have been found among artifacts of the Incas of Peru.

Genesis refers to Tubal-Cain, son of Lamech, as "an instructor of every artificer in brass and iron" (Gen. 4:22, A.V.). This account indicates that iron was worked from a very early period. Excavations have shown that iron ores were smelted in Mesopotamia in the third millennium B.C., for an iron blade dating about 2700 B.C. was unearthed there.

Probably the earliest iron used was meteoric iron. However, another theory advanced suggests that iron was first discovered in the ashes of a large fire built near red paint rock. When primitive cultures realized that the fire and paint rock were associated, and that iron had been formed by a combination of the two, fires were purposely built in such locations and the fires vigorously fanned by bellows, an early mechanical discovery, to melt out the iron.

There is no doubt that a considerable amount of meteoric iron may have been available. Meteorites have been venerated in religious ceremonies and enshrined in temples throughout the world and over a long period of history. The Ephesians worshiped Diana and the "thing which fell from the sky," no doubt a meteorite.

A German authority, physicist E. F. F. Chladni (1756–1827), in 1794 criticized scientists who ridiculed the possibility of such phenomena as meteorites, saying it was impossible for iron to fall from the skies. Then in 1803 a shower of meteorites fell at L'Aigle, not far from Paris. The objects which had been ridiculed now convinced the French Academy scientists of the reality of metal from the skies. Thomas Jefferson, scientist as well as statesman, skeptically discussed a reported meteorite fall in 1809. He explained that he would rather believe that the two well-known professors making the report were lying than believe such stones would fall from heaven!

As bronze tolled the death knell of the Stone Age, so iron foreshadowed the passing of the Bronze Age.

32. JACINTH

Jacinth: the nearly pure orange color of gem zircon; in the Bible is synonymous with hyacinth.

And the foundations of the wall of the city were garnished with all manner of precious stones . . . the tenth, a chrysoprasus; the eleventh, a jacinth, the twelfth, an amethyst. Revelation 21:19–20, A.V.

It must have been a most potent stone to be dedicated to the myterious dragon supposed to be responsible for eclipses of the moon and sun! The gem had incredible power, and its possessor was assured of certain victory over the spirits of evil that bedevil the human heart. It was the favorite stone of travelers, giving protection from two dreaded dangers faced by wayfarers of old: wounds and plagues. Certainly travel was exceedingly perilous in those times, and fearful men would be heartened by anything that promised security. In addition, the wearer was assured of a hearty welcome at any inn at the end of the day's journey, and the stone would augment his worldly possessions. The stone was jacinth, likely a garbled form of "hyacinth."

"The foundations of the wall of the city were garnished with all manner of precious stones. The first foundation was jasper . . . the eleventh, a jacinth" (Rev. 21:19–20). Only *The New Testament in Modern English* mentions zircon, the modern name replacing the archaic, discarded term "jacinth." In the Revised Standard Version, where instructions are given for the making of the breastplate for Aaron, jacinth is named in place of ligure as the seventh stone (Exod. 28:19). One wonders if the translators of the Revised Standard Version called the stone "jacinth" to agree with modern terminology for the yellow or orange-hued zircon. The Authorized Version had named this gem ligure, believed to be a yellow stone.

When an American diplomat's wife started housekeeping in Thailand a quarter of a century ago, she had an interesting experience. Having a large fishbowl and numerous tropical fish, she wished to obtain a quantity of brightly colored pebbles to make the bowl more attractive. Knowing these might be found on the banks of a nearby river, she offered a small coin to each of a group of native boys for a handful of the colorful stones. A few hours later she had almost a half-gallon of the tiny, stream-worn rocks at a cost of less than fifty cents. They ranged from colorless, yellow, orange, reddish-brown, and light blue to a very dark blue. Later, much to her amazement, she learned that practically every pebble in her fishbowl was a gem zircon.

Zircon is one of the oldest known gemstones. Much of its history remains a mystery. Its name is believed to have been derived from the Arab *zargun* (zircon). Zircon's composition was unknown until 1789, when scrupulous chemical analysis revealed its true nature. By that means, man was introduced to the element zirconium and the rare related element hafnium.

Zircon occurs in several colors, though not in as wide or complete a suite as some other gem minerals such as corundum or tourmaline. In hue, zircons range from glowing red, serene green, dazzling golden yellow to orange, starlight blue, and water-clear. The colorless jewels are close rivals of the diamond, for they have decided brilliance and luster and an intense inner fire. Zircons in all shades were widely used by ancient craftsmen for carving. These artisans of the Mediterranean area probably secured the gems from sources in the Far East (old Indo-China, Burma, and Ceylon) by way of trade routes to India. Ceylon has been known for ages as a veritable storehouse of gems, and gravel deposits found there have furnished practically every species of precious gem except the diamond.

However, the Greek term *huakinthos* used in Revelation 21:20 as in the Septuagint, corresponding to the Latin *hyacinthus*, appears to have been the blue sapphire. If jacinth is synonymous with hyacinth, we must con‧sider it a blue stone described in the foundations of the New Jerusalem. Writers of ancient days consistently used *hyacinthus* as descriptive of a shade of blue, as was *huakinthos*.

See Hyacinth; Ligure; Zircon; Lapis Lazuli; Sapphire.

33 · JADE

Jade: a tough compact gemstone; usually green, although it appears in several other colors; takes a high polish; a general term for two minerals, nephrite and jadeite.

Make the breast-piece of judgment; . . . Set in it four rows of precious stones: . . . the second row, purple garnet, lapis lazuli and jade. Exodus 28:15, 17, 18, N.E.B.

There is no one mineral called jade. The term "jade" is properly applied to two minerals which belong to entirely different mineral families, nephrite and jadeite. Nephrite is a variety of the amphibole actinolite. Jadeite is a member of the pyroxene family. The usual green color of jade is due to the presence of iron. Jadeite is harder, but nephrite is tougher (a real distinction) and more resistant to fracture. Chloromelanite is a rare exceedingly dark green to black jadeite containing additional iron. But the term "jade" is accepted for all.

Jade (jadeite) forms deep within the crust of the earth at depths as great as 20 to 30 miles under enormous pressure. Since rocks which have been under such great heat and pressure are not ordinarily found on or near the earth's surface, jadeite is rare. When it is found, it is evident that buried areas of great depth have been uplifted and the remaining cover over the jade removed through erosion. In a pure state both jadeite and nephrite should be white, a variety so rare that the Chinese considered it priceless. Chloromelanite is usually an intense greenish black. Between these two extremes is an endless array of colors, a result of the presence of impurities. The irregular distribution of color imparts a mysterious individuality to each piece. Jade is believed by the Chinese to have been forged from a rainbow to make thunderbolts for the storm god.

Impurities such as magnesium, calcium, and iron oxides give jadeite its wide scope of color. When chromium appears as an impurity the stone is called imperial jade and approaches an emerald-green color. The jadeite called mutton-fat jade is a treasured color. Other unusual colors are mauve, red, and bright yellow, found as scattered patches or streaks with colors less desirable. Jadeite is cryptocrystalline, an aggregate of minute crystals which are so closely interlocked that it is extremely tough. It has a vitreous (glasslike) luster when cut and polished, though the rough stone appears dull and waxy. Burmese deposits furnish most jadeite.

Since jade has been found in a number of archaeological digs in Bible lands, it must have been a familiar gemstone of early cultures. The only reference to jade by name which we have seen is in *The New English Bible.* However, *The International Bible Encyclopedia and Concordance* printed in 1908 suggests that "jasper" as used in the Scriptures might well be translated jade in many instances. In Revelation when jasper "clear as crystal" is mentioned, fine translucent jade could be the gem to which it refers (21:11). Jasper, the familiar quartz gem, is an opaque stone. (See Jasper.)

Merrill F. Unger explains that considerable uncertainty is found regarding the Greek term *iaspis,* usually translated jasper. Ancient peoples likely included lovely green jade as well as several hues of translucent chalcedony as *iaspis.* The Greek word often is used not so much to describe color or other special optical properties of the gem, but to indicate qualities of an object too beautiful to describe adequately. The delicate hues of jade with its translucency approaching the clarity of crystal might be the highly esteemed and cherished gem of the people of Bible days. (Also see Sard.)

Nephrite, the more common variety of jade, has a smaller color range than jadeite. It is really a very compact form of tremolite (actinolite, if green in color). The microscopic crystals of nephrite are hairlike fibers.

When the fibers are closely compacted, intertwined, and felted together the resulting material is the extremely tough nephrite. The dark-green variety called spinach jade is the most valuable nephrite jade.

Much nephrite jade comes from the Frazer River area in western Canada and from Alaska. A mountain of jade is mentioned in ancient Chinese legends. A great green gem of a mountain in the Kobuk River country above the Arctic Circle in Alaska is legend-like, too. Lieutenant Stoney of the United States Navy first discovered it in 1883. Its very lack of vegetation makes it appear green, for it is composed of bright green serpentine. In some areas of the mountain, nephrite is found, located in the very center of masses of undetermined material. Few people have ever seen unusual, majestic Jade Mountain in such a remote spot of our country. The discovery of jade here answers the "where" of material used by Eskimos for a long time in making adornments and implements of jade.

California also has famous nephrite deposits, and in recent years Wyoming has come to the forefront in the production of this gemstone, even exporting quantities to the Orient for carving. Found as loose boulders chiefly around Lander, nephrite also comes from the Laramie Range and the Red Desert.

Relics of jade prove that ancient races of both hemispheres used this exceptionally tough stone for weapons and crude agricultural tools. Natives of Central America and Mexico used it for religious purposes also. Scores of famous museums house age-old statuettes and ornamental carvings of jade.

Jade's hold on men of many races for centuries is difficult to explain. It was thought to link the mundane world with spiritual realms in Chinese philosophy. They believed a fragment of jade placed in the mouths of their dead gave them a heart "fresh and green." Such pieces of "tomb" jade are eagerly sought by collectors.

Many superstitions accompany jade, and it has been widely used as a good-luck stone. If worn on Fridays, it was believed to bring good fortune to the wearer. It supposedly protected one against ill health and was served finely powdered in drinks to royalty as a tonic. Confucius believed its greatest value was to remind man of the integrity of his mind and soul.

James Lewis Kraft, in his book *Adventures in Jade*, speaks of the naming of the stone on this continent ". . . by as curious a series of mishaps and misunderstandings as anyone could imagine. . . . Centuries after its classical glory in the Orient, the Spanish explorers in Central America found our early Indians using amulets of the hard, mysterious stone, firm in the faith that they could cure kidney diseases, and other quite earthy ailments. The explorers called these amulets 'pedra de ijada' (colic stone), and the French who followed them wrote it 'pedre de l'ejade.' A happy-go-lucky English printer decided to omit the Gaelic apostrophe and called it 'le Jade.' Jade it has remained."

34. JASPER

Jasper: an opaque, compact, cryptocrystalline variety of quartz, colored red, brown, yellow, or green by impurities; jasper of the Bible was probably a dark-green stone.

And thou shalt make the breastplate of judgment with cunning work; . . . And the fourth row a beryl, and an onyx, and a jasper; they shall be set in gold in their inclosings. *Exodus 28:15, 20, A.V.*

Jewish literature frankly admits that accurate determination of the names given the precious gems used in ancient times is extremely difficult, if not impossible. This is especially true in regard to the stones set in the high priest's vestments. The translators of the King James Bible were not gemmologists or mineralogists, and they rendered the Greek or Hebrew into the most familiar terms they knew. All the translations we have read list jasper as one of the breastplate stones, and all have placed it as the last stone of the last row except the Moffatt translation, which puts it in place of sardius as the first stone of the first row. A. Paul Davis selected a stone of yellow jasper and placed it in the more traditional place in the last row for his replica of the breastplate, but he used red jasper in place of sardius as the first stone.

Revelation has a vivid detailed description of the New Jerusalem which says in part, "And the city lieth foursquare, and the length is as large as the breadth. . . . And the building of the wall of it was of jasper . . ." (21:16, 18, A.V.).

In Scriptural times jasper was highly esteemed for gems, seals or signets, and small figures, and was much used. However, numerous stones were included which we do not recognize as jasper today. Modern terminology assigns opaque and richly colored varieties of chalcedony to jasper, especially those with shades of browns, reds, golds, and numerous shades of green. The Greek *iaspis* (jasper), according to descriptions by Theophrastus and later by Pliny, included several varieties of quartz of delicate color, many translucent, with rosy hues and several shades of blue and green, probably varieties of the gemstone called chalcedony today. Chrysoprase was likely included and jade also, as *iaspis* seems to indicate a gem of some rarity, and the many colors of modern jasper are neither translucent nor rare. The ancient manner of classifying stones helps to further confuse positive identification. For example, the Greek word *smaragdos*, meaning a green stone, probably included all green-hued stones from emerald to green jasper, including such varieties as chrysoprase, prase, plasma, bloodstone (heliotrope), aventurine, greenish-hued turquoise, and the lovely, rare jade. Many writers believe ancient jasper to have been jade. Egyptian jewelers of the fifth dynasty were expert at inlaying metal with rich blue and green stones, copper minerals. The green was malachite and the blue probably chrysocolla, but both materials are thought to have been called jasper by these artisans of antiquity.

Many strange powers were attributed to the jasper of old. It prevented sorrow, protected the owner from drowning, kept spiders and scorpions at a distance, and warded off ailments of the stomach, lungs, and chest. Drought, one of the dreaded blights of olden times, could be broken by jasper. Some believed it a remedy for snake bite, and others maintained that it denoted a state of "satisfaction."

Whether the ancient or the modern jasper, any one or all could have been used as a seal. In Greece and Rome seal rings were used to indicate ownership of property or rank or nobility, as they had been for many centuries. However, they developed a new custom of giving a ring as a token to show affection and regard. In early Rome, on the eve of a young woman's marriage, she received a ring from her father, given with love and affection for his daughter, but of very practical use, too, as it was engraved with the family seal. As mistress of her new home, she would use the seal on wine jars and food containers, and because they bore her seal, only she could open them.

Though most gemstones are not engraved in modern times, jasper remains a favorite material of the lapidary fraternity. The chalcedonic varieties of quartz, which include jasper, are cryptocrystalline or microcrystalline and are opaque or translucent rather than transparent. The material has a compact appearance and waxy luster. When the colors are intensely dark because of excessive coloring impurities, and the stone is virtually opaque, it is known as jasper. Being opaque, jasper depends on its color or pattern for its beauty. In Arizona's famous petrified forest the wood, which has been deplaced by jasper, displays a multitude of brilliant colors, blended and mottled beautifully. Occasionally a "scene" of trees or forest created by markings of maganese oxide can be found in jasper, which makes a lovely and unusual gemstone. The material takes a fine polish. Good, gem-quality jasper in many colors is found throughout America.

There is a brown variety, known as Sioux Falls jasper, from the locality which produces it in South Dakota. This stone was highly prized by the Indians for its color and is the jasper referred to by Longfellow in his poem *Hiawatha*:

> *At the doorway of his wigwam*
> *Sat the ancient Arrow-maker*
> *In the land of the Dacotahs,*
> *Making arrow-heads of jasper,*
> *Arrow-heads of chalcedony.*

35. LAPIS LAZULI

Lapis lazuli: a gem rock rather than a mineral name; an intergrowth of several minerals; has a rich ultramarine or azure blue color that makes it highly desirable for cabochon gems, mosaics, carvings, and inlays.

The foundations of the city wall were adorned with jewels of every kind, the first of the foundation-stones being jasper, the second lapis lazuli. *Revelation 21:19*, N.E.B.

The innermost case containing the mummy of King Tutankhamen of Egypt (ca. 1350 B.C.) is indeed a royal casket. Of solid beaten gold, it is decorated with the familiar triumvirate of gems so often used in ancient days. The colorful three are lapis lazuli, carnelian, and turquoise. Looking at the many recovered antiquities, one recognizes the predominance of these stones, especially lapis lazuli. Among the many treasures taken from Tutankhamen's tomb is one fabulous necklace of large scarabs carved from lapis lazuli, outlined in pure gold, and surrounded by intricate settings of carnelian, turquoise, and feldspar. Scarabs, images of the sacred beetles of Egypt, were regarded as symbols of immortality.

Lapis, one of the most sought-after and prized stones of ancient times, was used for personal adornment, seals, ornaments, and inlaying; finely ground, it was the paint pigment ultramarine. The tombs of the kings of Ur of Sumer, 1,100 to 1,200 years older than those of Nefertiti or Tutankhamen, reveal the use of lapis lazuli. Among the detailed objects found there is a goat standing upright with his forefeet against a flowering tree. The tree and head and legs of the goat are wooden with a gold overlay. The coat of the animal is made of shell, while his wide eyes and twisted horns are of lapis. Life in ancient Sumer has been vividly portrayed in "The Standard of Ur," an eighteen-inch-wide panel, one side of which depicts a battleground, showing the soldiers in battle and leading prisoners to the king. The other side pictures the king at a banquet while commoners bring gifts of all kinds. With lapis lazuli forming the background, the figures are inlaid with shell.

Egyptian jewelers a millennium later, who used gem materials lavishly, were masters at creating glass imitations of precious stones. The head-dress of King Tutankhamen's funerary mask has the typical blue stripes set in beaten gold. Genuine lapis would be expected. Instead, the inlays are clever, deceptive imitations made of deep-blue glass. Upon opening King Tutankhamen's inner coffin, archaeologists found 143 amulets and pieces of jewelry tucked in the folds of the many yards of cloth wrapping the mummy. Many were lapis lazuli.

In the early translation of the Scriptures, translators, using familiar terms, rendered the Hebrew *săppîr* as "sapphire." *The New English Bible* translates many passages relating to gems and minerals in terms which more nearly correspond to those substances actually known to ancient civilizations. Revelation 21:19 reads: "The foundations of the city wall were adorned with jewels of every kind, the first of the foundation-stones being jasper, the second lapis lazuli." Lapis had formerly been translated "sapphire." In Old Testament days lapis lazuli was a familiar available stone. The ancient, freely paraphrased version of the Old Testament, the Targums, telling of the life of the Jewish people, indicates that lapis may have been the material on which were inscribed the tables of the Law.

The *Encyclopedia of Bible Life* by Madeleine S. and J. Lane Miller suggests that the second gem of the second row of stones in the high priest's breastplate, while translated "sapphire" in the Scriptures, was probably lapis lazuli, and the replica of the breastplate made by A. Paul

Davis is adorned with a lovely gem of lapis in the place of sapphire. Most gems are classified as minerals, having a specific chemical composition and being of uniform material throughout. Lapis lazuli is a rock composed of several minerals. When magnified, an intergrowth of several minerals is seen, though it appears as a single mineral to the unaided eye. Lapis is an opaque stone, popular because of its intense blue color. The color is usually variegated, a blend primarily of blue, with gray, white, and gold interspersed. The blue color is due to hauynite or lazurite; the golden flecks are iron pyrite; and calcite gives the gray and lighter colors. The old Arabic term *lazward*, meaning blue, is the root from which come the names lapis lazuli, azurite, and lazurite. Lapis is softer than many gemstones, with a hardness of only 5.5, but its unrivaled hues of blue have made it a favorite material.

Pliny describes one beautiful mineral as being like the night sky spangled by stars, and Theophrastus describes a "sapphire spotted with gold." Surely they must have meant lapis lazuli!

In 1271, Marco Polo visited the extraordinary lapis lazuli mines of Badakhshan in Afghanistan, which have been producing gem material for 6,000 years. Persia has furnished some lapis, as has Bukhara in Turkistan. In recent years, fine material paler in color than the Afghan lapis has come from the Andes, at Ovalle, Coquimbo, Chile. Lapis lazuli of good color is found near the western end of Lake Baikal in Siberia, and upper Burma furnishes some material. In the United States sources of lapis are found in San Bernardino County, California, and on North Italian Mountain in Colorado. In the Albani Mountains south of Rome, on rare occasions small quantities have been found in the volcanic material thrown out by Mount Vesuvius, though this lapis is not suitable for gems.

36. LEAD

Lead: a heavy metallic element that rarely occurs in native form in nature; most common natural occurrence is in the compound with sulfur called galena.

The bellows blow fiercely, the lead is consumed by the fire; in vain the refining goes on, for the wicked are not removed. Jeremiah 6:29, R.S.V.

The Children of Israel, secure in their flight from the land of the Nile, sang a moving anthem of thanksgiving after their deliverance from a host of pursuing Egyptians. The racing chariots and myriad horsemen had been engulfed and destroyed in the churning waters of the Red Sea. Moses composed a psalm of praise, and Miriam the prophetess, Aaron's sister, took up her timbrel, urging the people to sing. Their song went thus:

> *Thou didst blow with thy wind, the sea covered them;*
> *they sank as lead in the mighty waters.* (Exod. 15:10, R.S.V.)

The Israelites were familiar with the mineral lead and its heaviness at the time of the exodus from Egypt, for Egyptian fishermen had long used the metal for sinkers in casting their nets.

Ancient ornamental medallions or coins of lead have been found in Egyptian excavations and ruins, and it is believed that man's working with and knowledge of lead predates recorded history. With its low melting point and the ease with which it could be reduced, lead was probably the first metal to be extracted from its ores through smelting by early man. Perhaps man built fires in pits close to outcroppings of ore to secure lead, as it is thought he did with iron at a later date.

Brought to Palestine by the Phoenicians from their far-flung voyages to Spain and beyond, lead came mainly from the "Tin Islands," the Cassiterides, a term referring to Great Britain, especially Cornwall. This mining area was long the main source of lead and tin for all Europe. Palestine also had a source of lead closer at hand, at Jebel e'Rossas, between Berenice and Kosseir near the Red Sea.

Lead in its native state is of rare occurrence. Although three or four primary ores yield practically all the metal, there are more than a hundred lead compounds. The main ore is galena, composed of lead and sulfur. The red oxide of lead, minium, known to the Hebrews, was used exclusively as a pigment. Their term for lead is derived from the Hebrew 'ŏphĕrĕth (literally, whitish), alluding to the mineral's grayish-white color. The Hebrews undoubtedly knew of a process for treating galena to obtain lead. Galena often contains silver, a probable source of that precious metal in Old Testament times.

> *The bellows blow fiercely,*
> *the lead is consumed by the fire;*
> *in vain the refining goes on,*
> *for the wicked are not removed.*
> *Refuse silver they are called,*
> *for the Lord has rejected them.* (Jer. 6:29, 30, R.S.V.)

These interesting verses indicate that the Hebrews had a very considerable knowledge of metallurgy, for lead was used as a flux, or alloy, in refining silver. Lead was a commonly used mineral in their lives, for Amos tells of the plumbline (plummet) with which God would measure or test his people, the line probably weighted with lead.

The unexcelled dramatist who wrote the Book of Job mentions lead as a writing material. Job, answering Bildad, exclaims: "Oh, that my words were now written! oh that they were printed in a book! That they were graven with an iron pen and lead in the rock for ever! For I know that my redeemer liveth . . ." (Job 19:23–25, A.V.). It is likely that a stylus was used to chisel the characters in rock, and molten lead was poured into the incised marks, though until archaeology definitely solves the puzzle, the method remains uncertain.

An important lead-producing area was at Laurium, Greece, though lead was less valued than the silver content of the galena ore. Mining may have begun here as early as 1000 B.C. Activity died down during the first century A.D., but the mines were reopened in the 1800's when deeper deposits were uncovered and found workable by modern methods.

The Romans made an almost modern use of lead, for pipes to carry water, and some of the pipe is still in serviceable condition. The Latin term *plumbum* means lead and gave us our word "plumber," one who lays water pipes or who works in lead. Pliny was one of the first writers to distinguish between lead and tin. Lead was frequently used to anchor great foundation stones together by pouring the melted metal into large holes drilled through the blocks. The towering Corinthian colonnade of the ruined temple of Bacchus at Baalbek, northeast of Beirut, Lebanon, gives dramatic evidence of this practice. Square holes in the columns show where Roman builders poured the fluid lead to lock together the massive stone sections. Centuries later, desert tribesmen removed the lead to make bullets.

The Egyptians had used a variation of this technique in the building of their gigantic pyramids. The huge granite or limestone blocks had dovetailed channels chiseled out vertically in a smooth face. Adjoining blocks were placed so the cavities met at the joint surface. Then molten lead was poured into the aligned openings to form a double tenon, firmly securing the great stones in place. The builders could thus dispense with using mortar. This method of fastening stone was also found in excavations conducted at Nineveh by Sir Austen Henry Layard.

Lead has long been used as a glaze for pottery. Ancient Assyrian and Egyptian glazes reveal the presence of oxide of lead when analyzed. A recent theory advanced by Dr. S. C. Gilfillan of Santa Monica, California, suggests that the use of lead in dishes and kettles may have contributed to the decline of the Roman Empire. Though lead poisoning as a cause of illness and death was unknown then, it probably caused the aristocrats to have a very low birth rate compared to the death rate. With the use of lead-lined pots and drinking vessels, and even lead-lined dishes; with cosmetics containing lead; and with the favorite color of paint in their homes being Pompeiian red achieved by the use of minium (red oxide of lead), the Romans certainly absorbed enough lead to poison them.

Galena (the main ore of lead) crystallizes in the cubic system. It has a high specific gravity, about 7.5, indicating its unusual weight, and has a grayish metallic luster. Other lead ores include cerussite and anglesite. These, with galena, are found in the United States, where the most important lead-producing states are Missouri, Idaho, Utah, and Colorado.

37. LIGURE

Ligure: a variety of precious stone that is likely a color variety of zircon, perhaps amber color; possibly an alternate name for jacinth or hyacinth.

And thou shalt set in it settings of stones, even four rows of stones. . . . And the third row a ligure, an agate, and an amethyst. *Exodus 28:17, 19, A.V.*

If you want to experience a real sense of frustration, try looking up "ligure" to get an idea of what mineral it really is! It is not even mentioned by accepted gem authorities; you cannot find it in mineral books that are considered the last word in authoritative definitions; and in many Bible dictionaries the stone may be barely mentioned but certainly not explained. *Unger's Bible Dictionary* attempts to shed light on the ligure and runs into the well-known confusion regarding the names of ancient gems, but it does present information from the past in trying to identify ligure.

Ligure, a translation of the Hebrew word *lĕshĕm*, is the equivalent of the Vulgate *ligurium*. *Ligurium* in turn has been associated with the

Greek term *lugkourion*, a stone identified by Theophrastus as a deep yellow gemstone said to be the solidified urine of the lynx. This yellow gem has been confused with amber, which it closely resembles in color; but unlike amber (a very soft stone with a hardness of only 2.5), *lugkourion* had sufficient hardness to wear well when utilized as a seal or signet. The hardness would indicate that it might be a variety of zircon (hardness 7.5) of amber color, indeed much like the hyacinth and jacinth of modern jewelers. Numerous specimens of seals carved from zircon can be seen in collections of ancient gems.

Theophrastus also described the stone as being "electric," attracting various bits of lightweight material to itself. Since this is a quality of amber, it aided in confusing *lugkourion* with amber. Amber is only one of several gems having this quality, however, the zircon being another, especially if heated or rubbed.

The concordance accompanying an 1895 edition of the Revised Version suggests that the Hebrew *lĕshĕm* and Latin *ligurius* is also the *lyncurium* of the Romans. The name possibly comes from Lunka, the native name for Ceylon, one of its chief sources, and may refer to the modern hyacinth and jacinth zircons.

Pliny speaks about the stone, though apparently doubting its existence; and he comments on statements made by other authors regarding it. He lists it following amber, for though it is neither electrum nor amber, all writers agree it is a precious stone. He says that both Diocles and Theophrastus agree that the ounce stone (*lyncurium*) has the same color as the "ardent amber resembling fire," and is a suitable material for engraving seals. A note accompanying Book 37 by Pliny, translated and compiled in *A Roman Book of Precious Stones* by Sydney S. Ball, reminds the reader that the properties of *lyncurium* strongly resemble those of tourmaline. Whatever the stone truly was, it was amber yellow, had electrical properties, and was hard enough to serve as a seal or signet. It may very well have been a variety of zircon.

The peculiar name for the amber-tinted zircon carried into the sixteenth century, for lynx stones were recommended as a cure for sleeplessness. (Insomnia does not seem to be entirely a product of the rapid pace of modern life!) One example is that of Cardanus, who in that century, suffering inability to sleep, carried a zircon in his pocket to induce the desired state, "which," he wrote rather doubtfully, "it did seem somewhat to confer, but not much." Some skeptical authors attribute his insomnia not to physical reasons but to a very temperamental blend of roguery and scholarship.

In the Exodus 28 quotation a number of varieties of gems are suggested by various translators for the first stone in the third row of the breastplate. The list includes ligure, hyacinth, and jacinth as this stone, as well as cairngorm (yellow quartz which tends toward a smoky hue), as translated by Moffatt; and A. Paul Davis selected golden sapphire for his replica of the breastplate.

38. LIME

Lime: a caustic highly infusible white solid, obtained by heating limestone or other forms of calcium carbonate; develops considerable heat when mixed with water.

And the people shall be as the burnings of lime: as thorns cut up shall they be burned in the fire. *Isaiah 33:12, A.V.*

How the great tower and massive walls must have glistened in the hot Palestine sun as David and his army approached the Jebusite fortress which was to be called Jerusalem! The face of the tower had been lime-washed, and parts of the walls had been thickly plastered with a lime mud. The dazzling whiteness of the small, triangular-shaped bastion was visible from far off. With valleys on three sides, the fortified city which David captured was less than eight acres, shaped like an enormous human footprint about 1,250 feet long and 450 feet wide. Because of its elevation, its never-failing water supply from the Gihon springs, and its tremendous walls, Jebus (Jerusalem) was considered unconquerable, but David's military prowess took it by storm.

Early cultures used lime in making whitening for the walls, the lime being secured by roasting limestone in kilns. The Hebrew words *'ăbnē gîr* (literally, stones of boiling) indicate the material used in making whitewash and various kinds of plaster and stucco. This Hebrew term is used in Daniel 5:5 (Moffatt), translated "plaster." "That very hour, the fingers of a man's hand appeared, writing on the plaster of the royal palace, opposite the lampstand." The Hebrew word *sîd* appears to have meant true lime, as used in Amos 2:1: "Thus saith the Lord. . . . I will not turn away the punishment thereof; because he burned the bones of the king of Edom into lime" (A.V.). Bone ash is lime.

The ancient lime kiln was a saucer-like depression or pit about three or four feet deep. Alternate layers of fuel and crushed lime rocks were placed in it. After the fuel was ignited, the kiln was covered with sod with an opening left to provide a draft, and thus lime was obtained.

Palestine is a land of limestone, deposited from seawater saturated with calcium carbonate (calcite). Limestone was also made up in part by the accumulation of shells or exoskeletons of small sea animals. Chemical analysis of some ancient mortars and plasters indicates that they were made of gypsum. Gypsum, also called sulfate of lime, is formed when a body of water without an outlet evaporates in a dry climate, leaving behind residues of various salts. Hydrous calcium sulfate, or gypsum, is one of these salts. Beds of gypsum are found along the Jordan River and in the Dead Sea Valley, so raw material for both calcined lime and calcined gypsum was available.

Whichever material was used, it remained waterproof and rock-hard even after 3,000 years. Cisterns, which honeycomb portions of the land, were lined with this substance, as were the gutters and channels diverting water into them. The coating on mud-brick houses and tombs and the plaster lining in sepulchers, probably a heavy whitewash or extremely fine mortar, were made of these minerals. We know that gypsum was the material used to make a plaster used on the pyramids of Egypt, pyramids which were built of enormous blocks of limestone.

The Scriptures refer a number of times to by-products of the two famous sources of lime, the sulfate of lime (gypsum) and the carbonate of lime (limestone). Moses commanded the people of Israel to remember the laws he had given them: "On the very day that you cross the Jordan into the land which the Lord your God is giving you, you must set up some large stones, and whitewashing them with lime, you must inscribe on them all the words of this code as soon as you have crossed, in order that you may enter the land which the Lord your God is giving you . . ." (Deut. 27:2–3, s.-c.).

In the lands around the Mediterranean, limestone was often used as a statuary material. When Sennacherib (704–681 B.C.) erected a new capital at Nineveh following the death of his father, Sargon, limestone figures on a huge scale were used.

Limestone was extensively used in building in Egypt. An outstanding example is the earliest free-standing stone structure known, the pyramid designed and built by I-em-ḥotep, counselor, architect, physician, magician, priest, writer, and composer of proverbs, for his king,

Djoser, who came to the throne about 2780 B.C. The pyramid tomb towers above the desert 190 feet. Fine white limestone from the Muqattam hills was used as the building material for the entire tomb and surrounding miniature city.

Limestone, the very skeleton of Palestine, was widely used in that land also for building, with much of the material enduring for centuries in the generally arid climate broken by variable wet seasons. Two seemingly identical blocks in an ancient wall may show one to be in good shape and the other badly decayed. The difference in condition may be due to various causes, including difference in age. Fortifications torn down during sieges and rebuilt from available material strewn about may have resulted in a stone's being laid next to one that was a thousand years older! Climate does strange, unpredictable things, easily seen when the stonework of the Hebrews is compared with that of the Egyptians. In Egypt, where the dry climate of the Nile Valley preserved even linen, papyrus, and delicate paintings, stones seemingly last forever; in Palestine, scarred by rigors of inconstant weather, the stones decay.

39. MALACHITE

Malachite: a vivid green, often banded, copper mineral which occurs with azurite; a hydrous copper carbonate.

The wall was built of diamond, and the city of pure gold, like polished glass. The foundations of the city wall were faced with all kinds of precious stone: the first with diamond, the second lapis lazuli . . . the eighth malachite. Revelation 21:18, 20, J.B.

A woman of ancient days found her cosmetic shelf laden almost as heavily as that of the modern woman. There were oils and perfumes for the skin, henna for tinting the finger and toe nails and for the hair, rouge for the cheeks and lips, kohl (powdered stibnite) for lining the eyelids, and colored powders for shadowing the eyes. One of the colors was a lovely green secured by pulverizing the copper mineral malachite.

Archaeology has revealed the widely accepted use of cosmetics and beautifying agents by both sexes, though especially by women, in all the ancient cultures. From the tombs of Ur, whose exquisite work in gold and silver developed even before that of the Egyptians, and from tombs along the Nile, cosmetic containers and aids of many kinds have been found. Delicate paint cups have been found in Sumer, while in Egypt a wealthy woman might have had a comb and hair curler, sticks for applying kohl to the eyelids, hair tweezers, bronze razor blades four to six inches long, and a beautiful mirror of bronze. Numerous little pots, jars, and cups of alabaster, ivory, and other materials have been found, as well as delicately carved cosmetic spoons, occasionally with the handles sculptured in the form of nude women, and tiny stone mills for grinding eye paint. Palestine has yielded up curling rods and ivory combs which date back to 1400 B.C.

The beautiful mineral malachite has many uses other than being powdered for eye shadow. Along with azurite and cuprite, malachite was one of the important copper ores mined in King Solomon's famous mines in the Wadi Arabah north of Ezion-geber, which helped to earn for Solomon the title of the Copper King.

Before Solomon's development of the copper deposits, the Egyptians, since about 4000 B.C., had mined the area located between Mount Sinai and the Suez. The Egyptians, who attached supernatural powers to many stones, used malachite as a child's charm to protect its young wearer from evil spirits.

Of all the minerals, none is more vivid or appealing to the eye than malachite and its companion mineral, azurite. Malachite, a bright, rich, almost emerald green, contrasts with the intense blue of azurite. Malachite gets its name from the Greek word for mallow, a plant whose leaves are somewhat like malachite in color.

Although malachite is usually recognized with ease because of its bright green hues, since it is a carbonate, a drop of acid on it causes it to effervesce vigorously. With its color, this definitely identifies it as the copper carbonate malachite. Usually found as a massive mineral, malachite is occasionally found in tiny needle-like crystals, to the delight of mineralogists.

Malachite has not been widely used as a gemstone, although its beauty indicates that it should be. The Romans made brooches of it; when framed in settings of gold, it made exquisite jewelry. Two factors have denied malachite its place as a popular gem. The first is its softness (only 3.5 on the Mohs mineral hardness scale), which makes it too easily scratched to be used as a ring stone. The second is its abundance, for it comes in large slabs and therefore is not an expensive material. The rarity of a gem helps to determine its desirability.

The beautiful boldly banded malachite, patterned with irregular concentric rings of darker tones, is a favorite ornamental stone, however. Large deposits of the mineral in the Ural Mountains of Russia supplied such quantities of the mineral that during the days of the czars it was made into vases, jars, jewel boxes, and even table tops! Many such articles, skillfully carved to bring out the pattern of the material and marked as gifts of the czars, are now housed in European palaces and museums.

In South Australia, the mineral has been mined in the old Burra Burra mines at Kooringa, and southwest Africa has also furnished fine specimens. The best-known American locality is the famed copper mines of Bisbee, Arizona. Here malachite and azurite occur together, making vivid specimens worthy of the finest collection.

40. MARBLE

Marble: a term loosely applied to any limestone, granular to compact in texture, capable of taking a polish; true marble more compact and crystalline owing to physical changes brought about by heat and pressure during periods of metamorphism.

And the merchants of the earth weep and mourn for her, since no one buys their cargo any more, cargo of gold, silver, . . . iron and marble. . . . Revelation 18:11, 12, R.S.V.

Many of the most beautiful buildings in the world are constructed wholly or in part of marble, the most beautiful rock in the world. The magnificent Temple of Solomon used it for superb ornamentation; the elaborate palace in Persia built by King Ahasuerus, whose queen Esther became, had flooring, inlays, and decorations of it; and Herod's restoration of the Temple in Jerusalem may have been of true marble. Noted throughout the world are other edifices of marble: the beautiful Parthenon at Athens, the exquisite Taj Mahal at Agra, India, and in our land the impressive Lincoln Memorial—examples of the beauty man has created of stone!

The name "marble" comes from the Greek *marmaros*, the equivalent of the Hebrew *shăyîsh*, meaning white. The Hebrew people used marble for ornamentation with a lavish hand, like other ancient peoples, engraving inscriptions and figures which have solved the puzzles and identification of many peoples, places, eras, and cultures. A piece of marble from an excavation in Caesarea, tentatively dated as late as the second to fourth century, proved to be a list of priestly Jewish families and the towns from which they came. The inscription referred to Nazareth, which had been doubted by skeptics as the home of Jesus. Nazareth is not mentioned in the Old Testament, in the Talmud, or in the writings of Josephus, but marble says the mountain village of Nazareth actually existed.

In the Old Testament we read of King David's amassing materials for the Temple which would be built by Solomon. Most versions list the materials he acquired similar to those in the quotation from the Authorized Version: "Now I have prepared with all my might for the house of my God . . . all manner of precious stones, and marble stones in abundance" (I Chron. 29:2, A.V.). Only *The Jerusalem Bible* translates "marble stones in abundance" as "masses of alabaster." Either might have been used for bas-relief carvings, inlays, statues, pillars, and flooring.

Some experts believe the walls of the Temple were built of limestone cut from a hill north of the Temple area. Others suggest fine Jurassic limestone, white or cream in color, from Lebanon. Its source is indicated in I Kings 5:13–18: "King Solomon raised a levy [of forced labor] out of all Israel; and the levy was 30,000 men. He sent them to Lebanon, 10,000 a month by division. . . . The King commanded, and they hewed and brought out great costly stones in order to lay the foundation of the house with dressed stone." An interesting note to this passage is given in *The Amplified Bible,* from which the quotation comes. The huge foundation stones described in the Scriptures still remain. One of them, enormous in size, almost 39 feet long, is considered one of the most interesting stones in the world and has Phoenician markings. Other authorities believe the enormous blocks visible in the Temple area of Jerusalem are remnants of the great platform upon which Herod's restoration of the Temple was built.

The Temple may have had a marble-like appearance, since the Hebrews made an extremely hard stucco of pulverized marble added to plaster which took a brilliant polish. Perhaps this was added to the Temple stones as a finishing coat.

Marble is a metamorphic, or "made-over," rock. The ancestral material from which it was produced was a calcareous (limy) mud, deposited in broad, shallow seas during several early geological periods. The mud was later compacted by pressure into limestone, then further compacted by heat and pressure (primarily pressure), and the limestone recrystallized to become marble. This recrystallization created coarser grains than those in the original limestone, giving more uniform hardness and grain. Some marbles (statuary marbles) are very fine-grained, however. The change from limestone to marble is less evident than observed in most metamorphic rocks.

Pure marble is a brilliant glistening white, and it has been used for ages as the material for magnificent statuary. Since marble yields readily to the sculptor's chisel and mallet, marble figures of tremendous beauty and vitality have excited the world's appreciation in many cultures. During the Renaissance period, Michelangelo (1475–1564), one of the greatest artists of all time, went beyond the mastery of anatomy in his figures to depict the spiritual struggle within man in the almost living stone. His overwhelming statues of Moses and David illustrate his superlative art.

Snow-white statuary marble comes from several locations. The Pentelic marble from Mount Pentelikon north of Athens, Greece, the Parian marble from the island of Paros, and the Carrara marble from Carrara, Italy, are world famous. The quarries at Carrara are the most famous quarries for any stone and are still in use.

Most marble contains impurities such as clay, sand, and iron oxide which were present in the original limestone and have been changed and redistributed to form the swirling patterns described as "marbling." "Marbles" in the broad sense exhibit a color range from white to black with any number of hues in between. In ancient times, and even today, the name "marble" is applied to any dolomite or limestone that takes a good polish. In the strict petrologic (rock science) sense, this is incorrect since these materials must undergo metamorphic changes to become a true marble.

Several sources of true marble are known in the United States, and the material has been used since colonial days. The Supreme Court Building in Washington, D.C., is a magnificent structure of marble, and the Boston Public Library is one of the finest examples of the use of matched marbles. Important marble-producing states are Vermont (with the largest American marble quarry), Tennessee, Missouri, Georgia, and Alabama.

One of America's most beautiful buildings, the Lincoln Memorial in Washington, D.C., is constructed of marble from three states. The 36 columns of the memorial, each 44 feet high and 7 feet in diameter, are of the fine white Yule marble quarried high in the wilderness area of the Rockies near Marble, Colorado. An enormous block of Yule marble weighing 56 tons was used for the memorial stone of the Tomb of the Unknown Soldier in Arlington Cemetery.

One of the largest blocks of marble ever quarried, weighing 93 tons, came from a Vermont quarry. The huge stone was made into a carving, *The Covered Wagon*, which reposes almost 3,000 miles from its place of origin, flanking the entrance to the Capitol in Salem, Oregon.

41. NITER

Niter: a nitrate mineral, a compound of potassium, nitrogen, and oxygen; often called saltpeter, an old popular name for niter; Biblical niter is an entirely different substance, natron.

For though thou wash thee with nitre, and take thee much soap, yet thine iniquity is marked before me, saith the Lord God. *Jeremiah* 2:22, A.V.

Solomon, sage as well as king, gave the world many wise sayings in his Book of Proverbs. One suggests: "As he that taketh away a garment in cold weather, and as vinegar upon nitre, so is he that singeth songs to an heavy heart" (25:20, A.V.). Certainly the words "vinegar upon nitre" were intended to show a reaction. Vinegar, the only acid known to the Israelites, poured upon the niter we know, would produce no reaction whatsoever!

Tacitus, in *The Histories,* mentions the use of niter in glassmaking. An eighteenth-century writer stated that ancient glass was made in the Holy Land by fusing niter with the sands of Palestine and Syria.

With our modern technology, we know these things cannot be. Our niter is saltpeter, potassium nitrate. Although of great value, it is not used for making glass, nor does it react to acid. Our niter is used in explosives and fertilizers. The niter of the ancients was natron. This substance, being a carbonate, would certainly effervesce if vinegar were applied (*The Amplified Bible* expresses the phrase as "vinegar upon soda"), and it was a basic material of glass. Our references to natron are to the substance translated "nitre" (niter) in the King James Version.

"Niter" comes from the Hebrew *nĕthĕr* or Greek *nitron*, terms for the substance we call natron. The form of the term we use, natron, was introduced into Europe about 1550 by two travelers in Egypt, Peter Ballon and Prosper Alpinus. It was meant to distinguish soda and potash (natron) from saltpeter (niter). Later, when the word "natron" was introduced into mineralogy in 1736 by Linnaeus, the term was applied to soda only.

A natural mineral alkali or soda, natron is sodium carbonate. It never occurs in nature as a solid material, only in solution, containing more than 60 percent water. When heat or evaporation remove much of the water, compounds containing varying amounts of moisture are produced in the form of a crusty alkali or deposit. One is much like our common "washing soda."

Natron is found in alkaline lakes in dry regions, and its ancient source was the Egyptian "soda lakes." Explorers described these lakes long ago, and Pliny and Strabo wrote of them. Located in the desert of St. Macarius, northwest of Cairo, nine soda lakes still provide large amounts of carbonates of soda mixed with various salts and sulfates. During the dry seasons, the small lakes completely evaporate, leaving a solid crust, and the large lakes lay down heavy deposits of salts rich in sodium carbonates. Spades and poles are used to break the crust into handling-size pieces. Dried even more on the lake banks in the hot desert sun, the crusts are taken to the Nile River for shipment to Alexandria.

Crete imports considerable amounts of natron for making soap. The ancients used these natural carbonates for washing and made a true soap by mixing them with oil. Natron, as a powdery carbonate, is used as a water softener in the East, making the hard limestone waters fit for drinking. But the same natron produces the "bitter waters of Marah," brackish springs which flow from soil impregnated with the carbonate.

People of ancient cultures, who also called the carbonate *nitrum*, *nitron*, and other similar terms, used the material in many ways, as we now use natron: for soap, salves, medicines, cosmetics, painting, and preserving food, in baking powder, and many others.

Natron was used in ancient glassmaking. Probably it was first made by one of the civilizations along the great rivers where ancient cultures began. Glassmaking may date back to 3000 B.C., possibly earlier, in Egypt, and *ca.* 2500 B.C. glass beads were made there. A rod of green glass from Babylonia, found at Eshnunna, may be a hundred years older, while at Eridu a small piece of blue glass dated about 2200 B.C. has been found.

The Egyptians, whose soda lakes supplied natron bountifully, used the material not only for ordinary glass but for making faïence, the oldest of all known glazed materials, 4,000 years old. Completely self-glazing, Egyptian faïence is relatively brittle, having no plasticity and containing no clay. Natron was mixed with ground quartz, one of its chief ingredients. Small simple shapes were modeled of it, or it was pressed into molds.

Natron was also used for embalming. Leftover natron, used in embalming King Tutankhamen, was discovered in excavating what must have been the funerary area where the body of the young king was embalmed. The material used to embalm the noble young body had been sanctified and buried, not to be used again. Just what it was and its use were unknown, and it remained stored in its containers at the Metropolitan Museum of Art in New York from 1909 until 1922, when Tutankhamen's tomb was opened. Then hieroglyphic inscriptions and seals finally identified the substance. The Texaco Research Laboratory analyzed it, listing the salts and carbonates and added organic materials such as herbs, myrrh, frankincense, and sandalwood. In embalming, after the removal of all major organs save the heart (believed to be the center of intelligence), the body was totally embedded in natron. Because of its affinity for water, natron removed all body moisture, making the corpse ready for the seventy-day ritual of embalming.

In the United States, alkaline lakes are found in California and Nevada, particularly Mono Lake and Owens Lake, where soda works have been built.

42. ONYX

Onyx: cryptocrystalline, chalcedonic quartz; flat parallel layers of different shades of color make it an excellent material for cameos.

The name of the first is Pison: that is it which compasseth the whole land of Havilah, where there is gold; And the gold of that land is good: there is bdellium and the onyx stone. Genesis 2:11, 12, A.V.

To many, the mention of a cameo brings a mental picture of the delicate face of a woman, but the first true cameos were portraits of a king. Imaginary figures of gods and goddesses had sometimes been depicted by Greek gem engravers, but the engraving of portraits of a living person was not attempted until the reign of Alexander the Great (356–323 B.C.). Alexander was a handsome youth with fine features and classic profile. It was he who began the custom of shaving because he did not want the splendid lines of his cheeks and chin hidden, and his portraits show him a beardless, young, even boyish, ruler. Onyx, with its flat, parallel bands of varying colors, was a perfect material for making the cameos.

Intaglio carving had its beginnings in the engraving of stones for use as seals. The cameo reversed the intaglio, as the cameo was raised and rounded—a face or figure cut in relief instead of being incised into the stone. Following the death of Alexander, when no longer only Pyrogoteles (his personal engraver) could etch the likeness of the royal face, many engravers cut intaglios or carved cameos portraying Alexander. Since the young king seemed to have been favored by fortune, the idea began to spread that owning a gem showing Alexander's features would bring good fortune to the wearer, and little cameos and intaglios became very popular.

Prior to Alexander's rule, onyx was used extensively as an incised stone for personal jewelry, especially in the form of a seal set in a ring. Aristophanes scoffed at the effeminate, gilded youths who loaded their fingers up to the nails with onyx seal rings, cut intaglio, and he also quoted Socrates, who had listed among the idle men of Athens: sophists, soothsayers, doctors, weather prophets, and "lazy, long-haired, onyx-ring wearers."

After Greece had been overpowered by Rome, Greek art continued to flourish, for the Romans admired their artistic efforts. Cameos especially increased in popularity, and portraiture on stone reached its peak during the time of Caesar Augustus, when his image was carved on onyx or similar material. Utilizing the layers or bands of color, masters of lapidary art could take full advantage of varying tones of color achieved by the thickness or thinness of the light-colored translucent layers which remained after the chisel had removed much of it from the dark, lower layers.

The word "onyx" comes from the Greek term denoting a fingernail. When cut parallel to the flat banding, onyx permits the dark underlayers to show through the semitransparent light-colored bands, suggesting the fingernail in appearance.

Onyx was used long before the Greeks became a great power, before civilizations as we know them even existed. Onyx stone was one of the first gems mentioned in the Scriptures, along with bdellium (whose meaning is uncertain, but we believe it was opal).

The Hebrews used onyx to make the shoulder stones on the ephod to which the breastplate would be fastened: "And thou shalt take two onyx stones, and grave on them the names of the children of Israel: Six of their names on one stone, and the other six names of the rest on the other stone, according to their birth. With the work of an engraver in stone, like the engravings of a signet, shalt thou engrave the two stones with the names of the children of Israel . . ." (Exod. 28:9–11, A.V.). In the breastplate itself onyx was used as the middle stone in the fourth row.

That the middle stone of the fourth row of stones in the breastplate might have been other than onyx is suggested in *The New English Bible,* in which this gem has been rendered as cornelian, while Moffatt translates it as beryl. The A. Paul Davis replica displays a golden beryl as this stone.

Another stone which is sometimes called "cave onyx" could have been the material used by the Hebrews. Dripping water from the ceiling of pitch-dark underground caverns made a kind of continual rain. Permeating the earth from the surface downward, it dissolved minerals and carried them along in solution. With its steady drip, the water deposited the minerals upon the uneven floor of the cavern. Through uncounted ages, a thick, solid layer composed of many bands of differing shades was built up. These bent, twisted, and curved irregularly, following the uneven contour of the cavern floor. The continual dripping also formed stalactites, stalagmites, and columns in the cave's depths. The banding in these, and in the floor deposits, made a desirable, very decorative material called "onyx" by people of ancient cultures. This material is not true onyx, but is travertine, a type of limestone. Found near Thebes, the stone is also called Egyptian alabaster and onyx marble. So the Hebrews had another beautiful choice for the gems used as fastenings for the ephod. We do not know which material was used.

Onyx is widely distributed and is frequently found in association with agate and jasper. In the United States, an extensive deposit was found in Madison County, Montana, occurring in a vein which extends for several thousand feet, with a surface outcropping. The onyx is of such fine quality that beautiful gems and cameos can be cut from it, and it has been mined commercially.

43. PEARL

Pearl: a dense concretion, lustrous and varying in color, formed as an abnormal growth within the shell of some mollusks, when of brilliant quality, can be used as a gem.

Again, the kingdom of heaven is like unto a merchant man, seeking goodly pearls: Who, when he had found one pearl of great price, went and sold all he had, and bought it. Matthew 13:45–46, A.V.

That gems could be thought endowed with mortal creature characteristics is hard to believe. But in olden times, pearl divers believed each pearl had a distinct personality and life. So firm was their belief that to them gems resembled human beings in some ways. Pearls could become ailing, lose their brilliance, and exhibit a lackluster paleness. This gave rise to a unique profession—that of pearl doctor! Unfortunately, no knowledge is available of his treatment or cures.

Prize pearls have an ethereal beauty and shimmering loveliness that beggar description. Delicate tints play upon iridescent surfaces ranging from gleaming silvery white, through several colors, to glistening black. The hues are so varied that one can find almost every color tint. Rarest of all are rainbow pearls, exquisite gems beyond duplication, which exhibit every hue and color of the rainbow.

To aborigines diving into sparkling tropical waters seeking the shellfish that might be hiding these elusive gems, pearls were known as gems of the moon. Great vitality was believed to be conferred on the finder. All pearls, even those of exotic form and color, were valued, but to find a rare, delicate rose-white or lustrous black pearl was truly a stroke of good fortune.

Clams and mussels, abalone and conch, and many other mollusks produce pearls. The outstanding provider is the pearl oyster, a variety much different from our edible oyster. There are many varieties of the *Pinctada* living in warm seas. Katherine Yerger Johnstone, in *Sea Treasure*, notes that the oysters vary in size from that of the hand of a baby to a large plate. The pearls which form range in size from tiny "seed" pearls to the largest pearl known—a huge misshapen mass weighing 14 pounds, found in a giant *Tridacna* clam near the Philippine Islands. In between are many sizes and shapes.

A pearl is formed when an irritant—any of many foreign substances, such as grains of sand, bits of shell, parasites, eggs of marine animals (perhaps of the oyster itself), or even mud—enters the bivalve, agape for food, and lodges within the tissue of the animal. The oyster, attempting to isolate the irritation and protect itself, covers the offender with nacre which hardens quickly. Successive layers of nacre are added like a painter brushing on successive layers of varnish. Of the oyster's effort to ease itself, a gem is born.

Natural pearls are sought around the earth. The Persian Gulf and Gulf of Mannar near Ceylon have furnished pearls for thousands of years. Beds near Australia, in the Sulu Sea, and around scattered islands throughout the Pacific are fished for pearls. Nearer the United States, the waters of the Gulf of Mexico, the Caribbean Sea, and along the western coast of Central and South America yield pearls. Freshwater pearls are found in the rivers of many lands, especially in the Mississippi and its tributaries.

Pearls have been known for millenniums. Civilizations which had their beginnings near the sea prized the pearl as a moon symbol, tranquil and beautiful, representing perfection. Worshiping the moon (believed to have been the first deity of ancient civilizations), these early peoples held its earthly symbol in highest regard.

The Sumerians and Egyptians probably were familiar with and used the pearl by 3000 B.C. It is likely that Egyptian pearls came from the Red Sea, where they were collected as late as the Roman period. The Red Sea is the source of an especially lovely pink pearl of rare beauty, greatly prized.

In the Old Testament references to the gem are uncertain, and only one comes to mind. Job says, "No mention shall be made of coral, or of pearls: for the price of wisdom is above rubies" (28:18, A.V.). Jewelry of Old Testament times reveals, however, that the pearl was known and used. While there are passages in the New Testament referring to pearls, there are not as many as one would expect. Perhaps one of the best known is from Matthew: "Do not give dogs what is holy; and do not throw your pearls before swine, lest they trample them under foot and turn to attack you" (7:6, R.S.V.).

There are many ancient tales regarding the pearl. One of these is a story of its origin. On certain days in the spring of the year when the sun shone brightly, oysters rose from the depths of the sea to the surface of the water. Here they opened to receive nourishment from divine sources, tears of the gods. The tears formed into pearls.

Other stories cluster about this inimitable gem. Cleopatra, the glamorous Egyptian queen, seeking to possess in her own person the incomparable beauty of the pearl, drank one dissolved in vinegar. History does not record the result! Another story is more probable. Cleopatra wagered with Marc Antony that at a single meal she could swallow the value of a whole province! Dissolving a pearl of great value in a glass of sour wine, she drank it. In reality such a large pearl would dissolve very little in wine. However, ground to a fine powder, the pearl could be swallowed in wine without injury.

For many centuries the pearl was known as the "Margaret," the Greek name for the lovely gem, a term used by the first translators of the Bible into English. One of the pearl oysters, named *Margaritifera vulgaris,* was known to ancient peoples, being found in the Persian Gulf and Red Sea. The King James Version discarded the Greek name and used instead the word "pearl," a literal translation of the Latin word meaning "little pear."

44. PITCH

Pitch: a black or dark-brown viscous substance obtained as a residue in distilling tar, wood tar, or petroleum, and occurring naturally as asphalt.

And the streams thereof shall be turned into pitch, and the dust thereof into brimstone, and the land thereof shall become burning pitch. Isaiah 34:9, A.V.

Pitch was man's earliest organic engineering material—its use as a cementing and waterproofing substance goes back to the dawn of civilization. Pitch served early man as a mortar between building stones, an adhesive with which to secure carvings and gems in place as ornaments, often on those same buildings, and a waterproofing agent for his boats as he set sail on unknown waters, going ever farther in his search for a better way of life.

In the King James and Revised Standard Versions of our Bible, the term "pitch" is used in but three references. First, before the great Flood, Noah was commanded by the Lord to waterproof the ark, pitching it "within and without with pitch" (Gen. 6:14). The second was when the little ark of bulrushes to hold the infant Moses was daubed with pitch. The third mention is much different from these. The Moffatt translation expresses it:

> All streams turn into pitch,
>   the very dust turns into brimstone;
> the land is a mass of pitch
>   that burns on, night and day. (Isa. 34:9)

The combustible qualities of pitch and the flammability of sulfur (brimstone) present a terrifying picture of punishment upon the wicked.

In older usage "bitumen" and "pitch" were used interchangeably and referred to the same substance. Biblically speaking, these two terms are used in five Old Testament passages, and the words "slime," "tar," and "asphalt" are used for the same or a similar material in various translations.

"Natural asphalt" refers to naturally occurring bitumens with silt, clay, or other mineral impurities. Such asphalt has long been called pitch, and it is found scattered over all continents. A few such occurrences are spectacular in scope. The famous 114-acre Pitch Lake on the island of Trinidad in the British West Indies and that near Lake Maracaibo in Venezuela are two of these. Lake Maracaibo was the source of pitch for calking the ships of sixteenth-century English and French pirates, who forced their way into the area to secure the needed material for their sailing vessels.

The world's largest known asphalt deposits, more extensive than the oil fields of the Middle East, can be found in North America. They are the Athabascan tar sands of Canada, and they cover an area estimated at 30,000 square miles.

Asphalt of several types is used commercially today, differing widely in origin, purity, and chemical constitution. One is Gilsonite or Uintahite, a natural substance of high purity, mined as a solid material. It is used extensively for making special lacquers in the insulation field and is found in veins in northeastern Utah near Fort Duchesne.

A second type comes from the natural but impure asphalts, such as the pitch lakes, and contains up to 34 percent colloidal clay. Another type includes the oil asphalts, called "artificial asphalts," widely used for paving, residues resulting from the refining of oil. Fourth are the "cracked" asphalts, by-products, but manufactured for specific uses, in petroleum-cracking operations. Last, there are the rubbery types, known as "blown," much used in roofing.

45. QUARTZ

Quartz: a combination of two elements, silicon and oxygen; the most common of all minerals; often found in six-sided crystals as well as masses of various colors.

The foundations of the city wall were faced with all kinds of precious stone: the first with diamond, . . . the seventh gold quartz. *Revelation 21:19, 20, J.B.*

A tramp mineral, it's called. That sounds like a rather sorry reputation, but actually the name isn't as bad as it sounds, for it really means that the mineral isn't exclusive in the company it keeps. That mineral is quartz.

Most minerals occur in specific geological situations or in association with special companion minerals. Not quartz! It is practically universal, found in formations of all geological ages and in many rock types. Quartz is one of the most common components of the earth's crust. It is present in almost every type of rock, igneous, metamorphic, or sedimentary. It is found filling cracks and crevices. It constitutes the largest part of nearly all sands and gravels.

The use of quartz has ranged from Stone Age artifacts to some of the most important building and scientific uses of modern man. Both concrete and glass are based on the use of quartz in the form of sand. The electronic engineer depends on fine crystal quartz as his source for oscillator plates.

A multimillion-dollar industry has been built on the 1880 discovery by Jacques and Pierre, famed Curie brothers, of piezoelectricity (from Greek *piezo*, pressure). In 1921 the additional discovery that thin slices or wafers of crystal quartz, properly oriented, vibrated mechanically at fixed radio frequencies made possible the stabilization of a radio transmitter's frequency. That one can tune to a radio station at a definite point on the dial is possible because of a small quartz wafer and an important observation by the young French scientists.

Quartz's sturdy composition, hardness, and tenacity give it strength and durability, and render it suitable for gem purposes. It varies from beautiful, well-shaped, limpid, water-clear crystals (rock crystal) to compact, deep-colored, smooth-surfaced jaspers. In contrast, it may be a rough, grainy compact mass of finely cemented crystalline particles known as quartzite.

Quartz crystal, cool to the eye as well as the touch, was used in ancient Rome by women of fashion to cool their hands in summer. They carried small crystal spheres or balls with them during the heat of the day. Propertius, Roman author (50–15 B.C.), wrote of his mistress, Cynthia,

> She'll now a fan of peacock's plumes demand;
> And now a crystal ball to cool her hand.
> Further she will pray
> For glittering baubles of the Sacred Way. (Elegy XV)

The "Sacred Way" mentioned was the jewelry quarter of Rome called the Via Sacra.

The use of lenses made of quartz crystal, begun in the early cultures of man, was continued for thousands of years. Sidney H. Ball, in *A Roman Book on Precious Stones,* tells of a unique use of quartz in the play *Clouds* by Aristophanes. The character Strepsiades wishes to evade a claim brought against him in the amount of five talents. He explains to a friend that he knows of a stone, transparent and beautiful, used for starting fires, which will solve his problem. By using the stone to concentrate the rays of the sun on the tablet of wax on which the court clerk writes, the charge would be "liquidated" as rapidly as it was inscribed.

While the pure mineral is colorless, quartz has many colors because of contained impurities. The names of many varieties are based on differences in color, such as amethyst and citrine. Quartz is affected by ultraviolet light and radioactivity. Radioactive disintegration is responsible for the color in smoky quartz.

The Moffatt translation of the Bible lists the first gem of the third row of stones in the breastplate as "cairngorm" (Exod. 28:19). Cairngorm is smoky quartz, the familiar six-sided quartz crystal ranging in color from a smoky yellow to dark brown or even black. In Scotland, where it is very popular, the gem is often used in pins, brooches, and other jewelry, and is regarded as the national stone. Deposits of smoky quartz in the Highlands at Cairngorm, Scotland, are almost exhausted. Smoky quartz of excellent quality comes from Ceylon, the Swiss Alps, and Spain. In the United States it is found at Paris, Maine, in New Hampshire, and in the Pikes Peak region of Colorado.

A record find of smoky quartz was made in 1868 in the canton of Uri, Switzerland. The amazing amount of approximately 3,000 pounds was found in a single rock cavity. Tourists descending from Galenstock saw dark areas in a band of white quartz about 100 feet above Tiefen Glacier in a precipitous rocky face. Their guide, Peter Sulzer, later was able to work his way to a cavity and collect some fine crystals. Adventurous collectors visited the locality still later and widened the passage to enter a larger cave which penetrated the mountain. Though filled almost to its ceiling with loose material, the cave had a great many beautiful smoky quartz crystals buried in it.

The gold quartz named as a foundation facing by *The Jerusalem Bible* (Rev. 21:20) may refer to citrine, a variety of quartz usually crystal in form and yellow in color, the hue being ascribed to ferric iron oxide. Its name comes from the Latin term for lemon but citrine quartz tends more toward brownish tones, though it may range from yellowish green through yellow to reddish orange.

Many of the 1,704 references in the Authorized Version to gemstones or implements are to varieties of quartz minerals, indicating their extensive use by the Hebrew people. Unmentioned are numerous other kinds of quartz gems, such as aventurine, which were likely available and used. The many hues—yellow, green, brown, and red—of aventurine make attractive gems, set off by their glistening scales of mica or hematite.

The lapidary, cutter of stones, of ancient Egypt was assigned an unusual job by the superb sculptors of those days. Their realism in portrait sculpture has never been exceeded, and the lapidary was assigned the task of making artificial eyes to be placed between the unblinking lids of the statues. The stone or wooden heads were painted in full and lifelike color, and the eyes of rock crystal with black pupils (perhaps obsidian) gleamed brilliantly.

46. RUBY

Ruby: a colorful precious stone, a distinctive red variety of corundum· often called the "true" or "Oriental" ruby.

And you must insert in it a setting of stones, four rows of stones, . . . the second row a ruby, a sapphire, and a crystal. Exodus 28:17, 18, S.-G.

A signet stone so warm that it melted the wax on which it was meant to leave an impression? Archelaus declared this was true of the ruby. When the glowing red gem was engraved and used as a seal, its fiery heat only melted the wax on which it was impressed, even though used in a cool and shadowy place.

As with most gems of ancient days, a number of strange beliefs were associated with the ruby, many because of its beautiful color. It was believed that the stone imprisoned a glowing spark, struck from the planet Mars, which would not dim or quench until the aging earth itself grew sere and cold. Many regarded the ruby as dedicated to high noon or bright midsummer, and believed it a shield against adversity. Others thought its suggestive warmth of color brought peace and contentment.

Many powers were attributed to the gem. Some wanted the ruby because it would guard their houses, orchards and vineyards, or livestock from tempestuous storms. An old legend tells of a king of Ceylon who owned a ruby five inches in diameter which he rubbed on his brow each morning to receive the gift of youth for that day.

Pliny, in his last book of *Natural History,* told of the use of various precious stones for palliative and occult purposes. Belief in the medicinal powers of precious stones persisted even to the time of the Medicis. When Lorenzo was dying, court physicians attempted to save him by administering a powder of crushed rubies, sapphires, and possibly other precious gems. Such medication probably only hastened his death.

In Egypt, ornaments placed on mummies were believed to warm the corpses by powerful emanations radiating from the gemstones set in them. This held true even though the gems were glass facsimiles, and whether the deceased was an ordinary person or royalty.

Ruby is an aristocratic member of a prosaic, workhorse, metal family which is one of the most abundant elements in the earth's crust. This metal is found in kitchen pots and pans, paint, auto parts, building panels, and countless other items. It is aluminum, one of modern civilization's most extensively used materials. An interesting tale is told of aluminum when it was a prized rarity almost a century ago. Napoleon III of France, enthralled by the new mineral, which was valued above even gold and silver, had forks and spoons made of it. The most esteemed guests at court banquets were given the aluminum tableware, while lesser-ranked guests received ordinary gold and silver cutlery.

Ruby is merely the deep-red form of aluminum oxide (corundum) which owes its color to traces of chromium. Nature has given ruby an incomparable color. Really fine rubies are so rare that they are worth more, carat for carat, than diamond. Some gemmologists rate them as the most expensive of stones. Ruby, so distinctive in color, has a name and classification entirely to itself. All other colors of the gem corundum are called sapphires; even pale-red stones are pink sapphires. As the color grades into deeper rose and darker red hues, the gem becomes ruby.

Rubies occur both in placer gravels and in metamorphic rocks. They are found in crystalline limestone, mica schist, basalt, and pegmatites. Ruby's color is so well known that "ruby-red" has become a descriptive term for that hue which has the slightest tinge of blue blended with deep carmine red. The gem's popularity lies in its color, for it lacks fire. It has long been the first choice of Oriental peoples, from which part of the world it first came. It makes a splendid gemstone, since only diamond is harder. Ruby (like sapphire) has no cleavage, though it does have a parting, and there is very little tendency to fracture.

Some rubies may show asterism when cut in rounded form (*cabochon*), exhibiting a six-rayed star in its rounded dome. The rays always appear white regardless of the color of the stone. This star effect is produced by either oriented needle-like inclusions (usually rutile) or a lattice-like formation within the gem. The inclusions which create the asterism prohibit complete transparency in a star gem, though clarity is desirable.

The largest known star ruby weighs 100 carats and is milky crimson in hue. The brilliant six-rayed star is especially well defined in this lovely stone found in Burma. Named for its donor to the American Museum of Natural History in New York, where it is displayed in Morgan Hall, it is called the Edith Haggin de Long Star.

Rubies of somewhat pale color are found in the gem-bearing gravels of Ceylon. In Thailand, at an area called the Hills of Precious Stones, quantities of darker-hued stones have been located. A 40-square-mile area around Mogok, Burma, has long been known as the source of the finest gems, providing most of the truly rare stones, especially those of the color known as "pigeon's blood," a deep red lightly touched by violet. Burma's lead in the production of fine rubies became so prominent that the king of Burma used to have the title Lord of Rubies and, as such, could lay claim to the finest rubies mined in his country. Some rubies of inferior quality come from Australia. In the United States small but fine rubies have been found in stream gravels of Cowee Valley in Macon County, North Carolina. Some have been found near Helena, Montana, along the upper Missouri River, with sapphires.

A remarkably large ruby was found in the southeast corner of Yugoslavia near the Albanian border. The 7,825-carat purplish-pink ruby, shown in color on the cover of the *Lapidary Journal* for September, 1969, is in Munich, West Germany, at the Bayerische Hypotheken und Wechsel Bank.

Red garnets and red spinels have often been regarded as rubies. The most famous example is the Black Prince's ruby. One Christmas season the Black Prince, son of King Edward III, was persuaded while visiting at Bordeaux to aid the Spanish king. The prince was promised a great treasure for his service. Winning the decisive battle of Nájera on April 30, 1367, his reward was a single red gem. Still one of the stones in the British crown of state, the gem is not a ruby, but a red spinel.

John Ruskin said of red spinel (believing it a ruby) that it was the loveliest precious stone of which he knew. Though Ruskin was a lover of beauty for beauty's sake, his statement might have been a little more subdued had he known it was spinel, for the name "ruby" denotes in itself superlative beauty. Before the day of the scientific mineralogist and gemmologist, the naming of precious stones was much simpler! For instance, any lovely transparent red stone was called ruby regardless of the mineral group to which it really belonged.

Only the Smith-Goodspeed version of the Scriptures lists ruby as a stone of the breastplate. It is the first stone of the second row. A. Paul Davis also selected the ruby for this gem on his breastplate replica. *Nōphĕk*, the Hebrew term for the gem assigned to this location, means "shining," and there has been a great deal of confusion as to the stone which should occupy this place. It is believed that the true ruby may have been known to the Hebrews but confounded with red spinel and garnet under the names of *anthrax* (a Greek term) or carbuncle.

In the Authorized Version of the Bible, in Proverbs, where wisdom is compared to rubies, the rendering of the term seems uncertain, and some more recent versions indicate red coral. The Hebrew terms *pänîn* and *pänî* do not indicate color, but only a comparison to precious objects or great beauty. Some students believe pearl might be a reasonable rendering. However, rubies, too, are objects of beauty and value, and are highly to be desired, as is wisdom (Prov. 3:15, 8:11, 20:15).

See Sapphire.

47. SALT

Salt: the mineral sodium chloride, used to season and preserve foods.

Ye are the salt of the earth: but if the salt have lost his savour, wherewith shall it be salted? it is thenceforth good for nothing, but to be cast out, and to be trodden under the foot of men. *Matthew 5:13*, A.V.

Nature's stockpile of elements contains a host of diverse characteristics. Many are gentle and easily handled. A few are so vicious that their use demands extreme care. One such element, chlorine, is a heavy, greenish-yellow irritating poisonous gas. Another, sodium, is a soft, silvery-white substance so chemically active it must be kept immersed in oil to prevent its catching fire from rapid oxidation. Strangely, when these two noxious elements, chlorine and sodium, combine, they form common salt, a beneficial mineral of fascinating history and one of man's most versatile servants.

Salt is found in sedimentary rocks of all ages, widely distributed throughout the world. Near Ithaca, New York, seven huge beds of salt total 250 feet thick. These great, interbedded, precipitated salt bodies are called rock salt, and in some areas of the world the beds are as thick as 2,000 feet.

The deposition of one cubic foot of salt requires the evaporation of at least eighty cubic feet of normal seawater. Such extensive thickness indicates that desert conditions with intensive evaporation existed here for a very long time. Ohio, Louisiana, Michigan, and Kansas have considerable salt deposits, and the Great Salt Lake and the saline lakes of southern California also furnish the mineral.

A great many salt mines are operated today around the world. One of the most famous is also one of the oldest, having been worked for centuries. The miners have served as sculptors, carving out chapels and galleries and many kinds of monuments in the enormous beds of rock salt. In the airy, dry, sparkling man-made caverns of this mine at Wieliczka, Poland, stand many statues which must remain where they are carved, for the humid air outside the mine would destroy them.

Salt mines of Austria and northern Italy acted as safe repositories for plundered art works from galleries all over Europe. Near the end of World War II Nazi art thieves hid many priceless works of art in the airy mines. Because of the constant temperature and low humidity, no damage came to any of the works during their considerable period of storage there.

Infrequently salt occurs in lustrous, white cubic crystals in salt waters subject to rapid evaporation. The creation of such crystals happens at midsummer at the sacred salt lake of the Zuñi, south of their pueblo in western New Mexico. Winds carrying salt-laden moisture from the lake deposit the salt on all vegetation growing near. Soon every blade of grass and weed becomes a mass of small, gleaming white crystals. By wading into the lake at this season of the year, large groups of crystals—often imperfect, however—can be recovered.

In ancient Greece, salt was traded for slaves. When a slave proved unreliable or lazy, he was described as "not worth his salt." The word "salary" comes from the Latin *salarium argentum*, a name Roman soldiers gave to the special ration of salt received as part of their pay.

Salt (the Hebrew *mĕlăh*) abounds in Palestine, the Dead Sea being one source, but it was secured more easily from Khashin Usdum, a rock salt cliff extending nearly seven miles along the southwestern shore of the sea, than by evaporating it from the salt waters. Salt was used in religious observances in both vegetable (Lev. 2:13) and animal (Ezek. 43:24) sacrifices.

The Dead Sea is not referred to anywhere in the New Testament, and in the Old Testament it is called Salt Sea, Sea of the Araba, Sea of the Plain, East Sea, and Former Sea. Pliny called it the Sea of Asphalt, and Josephus called it both the Sea of Asphalt and the Sea of Sodom. It is the most striking and remarkable geographical feature of Palestine. Fifty miles in length and less than ten in width, it has no outlet to the south but receives the flow of the Jordan River from the north. Tremendous evaporation is caused by the intense heat of its location and its great depth below the surrounding land. Evaporation is so rapid that it counterbalances the inflow of water from the Jordan and a few small side streams and maintains a constant water level. It lies 1,286 feet below sea level, and rugged mountains higher than 2,500 feet wall in the waters on the east, while high cliffs bulwark the west. So salty is the sea that fish perish in a matter of minutes when leaving the waters of the Jordan. It contains up to 25 percent mineral content compared to 5 percent for the Atlantic. Taking advantage of the minerals in the bitter waters, modern Israel has built two up-to-date plants to extract phosphates and bromides. The phosphates are used for fertilizers and the bromides for medicine and photography, their sale making an economically valuable resource.

Rites of friendship and protection have been connected with eating together. Since salt was used in the food, a "covenant of salt" meant a perpetual covenant. In 1854, during the great Indian mutiny, only the Sepoy tribes remained loyal to the British crown. They had sworn allegiance "by their salt," a binding oath. Salt also symbolized fidelity.

Frequent Biblical references are made to salt's usefulness, literal and figurative. Its medicinal qualities were known, for the prophet Elisha used salt to remove a plague infesting the water supply of the city of Jericho (II Kings 2:19–22). Salt is often used as a symbol of perpetual desolation. An excess of salt and other saline substances on and in the soil makes it sterile, demonstrated by the utter barrenness of the land surrounding the Dead Sea: ". . . and salt-pits and a perpetual desolation" (Zeph. 2:9). "And the whole land thereof is brimstone, and salt, and burning, that is not sown, nor beareth, nor any grass groweth therein" (Deut. 29:23). Lot's wife was turned into a pillar of salt when she disobeyed God by looking back at the destruction of Sodom and Gomorrah, cities on the Dead Sea (Gen. 19:24–25).

We who are accustomed to high standards of purity in modern products may not comprehend the full implication of the words about salt which Christ spoke in his Sermon on the Mount. He said, "You are the salt of the earth, but if salt has lost its taste—its strength, its quality—how can its saltness be restored? It is not good for anything any longer but to be thrown out and trodden under foot by men" (Matt. 5:13, A.B.). How can salt lose its saltness? The explanation is reasonable and simple! Ancient salt contained clay or other impurities such as gypsum, which alone remained after the salt had leached away, though the material retained its original appearance.

Minerals and Man by Cornelius S. Hurlburt, Jr. has an account of an ingenious method of stealing such salt. Salt, probably second only to flint in helping establish trade routes, was carried in large amounts in caravans following the ancient trails. This salt, too, contained a great amount of impurities. Clever thieves removed the salt in such a way that it was not soon discovered. The bag containing the impure salt was soaked in water, and the salt dissolved into the water, to be reclaimed later by the thieves through evaporation. Meanwhile the supposed salt reached its destination, where the merchants discovered that only a tasteless residue remained. The salt indeed had lost its savor.

48. SAPPHIRE

Sapphire: a pure variety of corundum in transparent or translucent crystals used as gems; the name used for corundum of any color except red, which is called ruby; usually thought of as blue in color.

And this is how I saw the horses in my vision: the riders wore breastplates the color of fire and of sapphire and of sulphur. *Revelation 9:17, R.S.V.*

The Hebrew Talmud relates the legend concerning the miraculous stone called the Shämîr, with which Solomon trued the stones of the Temple. The Shämîr, a magical gem or instrument, had also been used by Aaron to cut the stones for the breastplate of the high priest. Solomon had been instructed to build the Temple without the sounds of hammers, which made it impossible to cut the building stones in the ordinary manner. But by laying the Shämîr against the side of the rock, the stones were instantly and noiselessly separated according to any desired pattern.

The word "sapphire" has the same confusion existing around it that is found regarding other Bible gems. The Hebrew word *săppîr*, meaning "something engraved upon," is translated "sapphire" in early versions of our Bible. However, sapphire, second only to the diamond in hardness, is a material too hard to be engraved with ordinary tools. Later translations render *săppîr* as "lapis lazuli," a material much easier to work. In the New Testament sapphire is referred to as jacinth (and sometimes hyacinth), and the *hyacinthus* of the Romans and *yacut* of the Arabs refer to the modern sapphire as we know it. But modern hyacinth is ligure or jacinth, all three terms being just other names for the orange, reddish, and brownish transparent varieties of zircon. Yet hyacinth can also mean the cinnamon-colored variety of garnet. Puzzling, isn't it? One conclusion we can reach is that the true sapphire was evidently not known in Old Testament times, and when the Scriptures mention sapphire, the deep-blue, opaque lapis lazuli is meant; but sapphire was known by New Testament times and was called jacinth or hyacinth.

At just what step on the ladder of history the true sapphire became known is uncertain. Today nearly everyone is familiar with the famed member of the gem corundum, of beautiful cornflower blue, which ranks with diamond, emerald, and ruby as the "precious stones." Other sapphires vary from clear, light pink, yellow, orange-brown, and green to a lovely lavender strongly resembling amethyst. Only the red sapphire has a special name, ruby. Several colors may be seen in adjacent layers in a single crystal, and some of these are cut into striking and unusual gems. A carving of Confucius is made from a sapphire in which the head is colorless and the body pale blue with yellow legs, all from a single stone.

Corundum is aluminum oxide and when pure is colorless. Frequently a part of the aluminum is replaced by tiny amounts of other elements such as chromium, iron, or titanium oxides, and these are sometimes credited with the various colors. Chromium is believed to create the red hues, and titanium and iron the blue. Sapphire is extremely hard, has no cleavage, and has little tendency to fracture. Some sapphires show asterism, the six-rayed star, always white regardless of the stone's color. These are the much desired star sapphires, long cherished because of the belief in their virtue of being able to conquer all the forces of evil. The most famous of all star sapphires is the Star of India, an enormous blue-gray *cabochon*-cut stone weighing 563 carats. It is housed in New York at the American Museum of Natural History, Morgan Hall. In 1964 the Star of India and several other beautiful and famous stones were stolen. Most of them, including the Star of India, were recovered.

Sapphire mines are usually open pits, and the methods of recovery are somewhat primitive. The gem-bearing stream-bed deposits are washed much the same as in hydraulic mining or sluicing for gold. The mines in upper Burma, worked since the fifteenth century, yield the finest, although the sapphires from Thailand are a close second. At present, Thailand furnishes nearly half the world's supply of these gems, though the late 1960's have seen increased activity in mining the Australian sapphire-bearing gravel. The Australian sapphires, though they exhibit a rich blue color when viewed in natural light, appear black when seen under artificial light. Kashmir, in northern India, has long been famous for its superior gems which maintain their rich color in any light, but the deposits seemingly are now exhausted. During the nineteenth century the finest and most beautiful of sapphires came from Kashmir, and these gems are the measure for sapphire's finest color. Ceylon's gem gravels produce numerous fine and desirable stones of many colors, though often paler in hue than those of other localities. Other important sources of sapphires are Afghanistan, China, Hindustan, Queensland (Australia), and the Ural Mountains of Russia. The best sapphires in the United States are found in sandbars along the upper Missouri River near Helena, Montana, especially the El Dorado bar and in Yogo Gulch, and in gold washings on the Judith River. In North Carolina most gems are mined at Corundum Hill near Franklin, in Macon County.

Several large sapphires have been found. A Buddha carved from a single sapphire is housed in the British Museum. A sapphire belonging to an Oriental king (whose great treasures were lost) was long considered the largest of this gem variety. Even this almost legendary stone was surpassed in size by a sapphire named the Gem of the Jungle. During a severe storm, lightning caused a tree to fall, uprooting it. Formerly concealed by its roots, the Gem of the Jungle, weighing 958 carats, was exposed. The stone, purchased by an American for more than $100,000, was cut into nine lovely gems. The largest of these weighed 66 carats.

Harry and James Kazanjian, gem dealers of Los Angeles, California, recently presented four of the most unusual sapphires known to the Smithsonian Institution in appreciation for the opportunities given them by America. The four sapphires, three blue-black ones and one black, have been carved with the heads of four Presidents, Washington, Jefferson, Lincoln, and Eisenhower. Of the four, the largest is the gem engraved with the head of Lincoln. The dark-blue sapphire, the largest known, weighing 1,318 carats (9 ounces), came from an Australian mine. The carved head of the sixteenth President is 2 ⅜ inches high, 1 ¾ inches wide, and 2 inches deep.

An age-old tradition, widely believed by some Oriental peoples, maintained that the earth rested upon a gigantic blue sapphire, with the bowl of the sky mirroring its radiant blue. Certainly today that blue reminds men of cosmic space. Others believed the gem attracted divine favor when worn as a talisman, and it was considered Saturn's stone. It was thought that the celestial throne of judgment stood upon the sapphire.

The natives of Ceylon thought the powers of the sapphire remained with the original owner, even if it had been lost, sold, or given to another. The sapphire was also favored as a love charm by ancient people. Gems of the classic, deep, sky-blue color were always held as stones of wisdom. Whether legends or beliefs were attached to the other colors of sapphire, the "fancy" gems, is unknown.

Traditionally, in ancient writings, sapphire was considered the stone upon which the Ten Commandments were inscribed, but because of the size required of tablets which contained God's laws for men, lapis lazuli was probably the stone meant.

Several translations of the Bible indicate an awareness of lapis lazuli as the stone denoted by *săppîr*; footnotes and marginal notes mention that lapis was probably meant rather than sapphire. *The Jerusalem Bible*, though assigning sapphire as a breastplate gem, translates one of the facing stones of the foundations of the New Jerusalem as lapis lazuli. In the Authorized Version, the passage quoted at the beginning of the article reads ". . . having breastplates of fire, and of jacinth, and brimstone," while the Revised Standard Version translates "jacinth" as "sapphire." Since this passage is one of New Testament times, sapphire seems a logical rendition.

Though almost all versions translate the center stone of the second row of gems in the high priest's breastplate as sapphire, A. Paul Davis selected lapis lazuli for his replica. Sapphire is also named as one of the gems in the covering of the Prince of Tyre (Ezek. 28:13) and as a facing of the foundation stones of the New Jerusalem (Rev. 21:20) in some versions of our Scriptures.

49 · SARDINE STONE

Sardine stone: likely an alternative name for sard, a quartz mineral.

. . . and, behold, a throne was set in heaven, and one sat on the throne. And he that sat was to look upon like a jasper and a sardine stone. . . . Revelation 4:2–3, R.V.

How difficult it is to put into words something of almost indescribable beauty! St. John, in his vision described in Revelation, must have searched for adequate words to share with others the glory and loveliness of God upon his throne. "And he that sat was to look upon like a jasper and a sardine stone" (Rev. 4:3). The jasper might well have been jade of superlative quality, and the sardine stone, if sard, must have been of rare color hue, perhaps rich chestnut brown, of great fineness and translucency. What a stunning contrast would be made by these two beautiful gemstones, of such different color, and both held in such high esteem by ancient peoples.

Though most Biblical authorities believe sardine stone to have been only another name for sard, it is not definite, as pointed out in *Unger's Bible Dictionary*. The Latin *sardius*, used in Revelation 21:20 as a stone decorating the sixth foundation of the New Jerusalem, is not the same as that translated "sardine stone" in Revelation 4:3, the Latin being *lithos sardinos*. It may have been the same mineral, but an uncommonly beautiful variety.

The wide usage of sard, and also of jade (or jasper), as materials for signet seals might have caused them to be the gems selected by John to describe the One who sat upon the throne. In Revelation 7:2-8, John tells of the "seal of the living God," bearing the name of God engraved upon it. The impression of the seal upon the foreheads of the faithful symbolized safety and deliverance from judgment for the servants of God.

We do not know the nature of the mineral of the seal described thus in the vision. We do know that sard, the gem chalcedony, in hues ranging from yellow brown through red brown, has been found widely, from Egypt to India, in its use as a seal.

The Biblical story of the Jewess Esther, queen of Ahasuerus (perhaps Xerxes, son of King Darius), who through her favor with the king saved her people, shows the dramatic use of the seal. Haman, prince of the court, had ordered the Jewish people destroyed. His letters, sent throughout the kingdom, had been stamped with the seal of the king. In undoing the catastrophe about to befall the Jews, Esther used the ring seal, now given to her by King Ahasuerus, to impress letters preventing the slaughter. Documents of ancient Persia were sealed in two ways: with a cylinder seal if written on tablets of clay or with a signet ring if written on papyrus.

In days of antiquity a seal's impression had the same validity as an actual signature. The custom continues today in some areas of the East, and the impression of a seal on a document came to have such importance that even now many documents are not considered authentic without a seal affixed.

50. SARDIUS (SARD)

Sardius: a deep-orange to brownish-red variety of chalcedony, classed by some as a variety of carnelian.

The foundation stones of the wall of the city were ornamented with all kinds of precious stones. The first foundation stone was jasper . . . the sixth sardius. *Revelation 21:19–20,* S.-G.

A staff and a signet ring were essential accessories for the fashionable man of ancient days. Herodotus relates that every Babylonian man carried a seal ring and a staff, the head of which was ornamented with a carved figure of a flower. Evidently the custom was adopted by the early Israelites, for in Genesis 38:17–18, Tamar asks, "Wilt thou give me a pledge?" and Judah replies, "What pledge shall I give thee?" Tamar answers, "Thy signet, and thy bracelets and thy staff that is in thy hand." These articles, and the ornament on the staff, were probably made of sard.

Sard was especially popular for seals because, as with other chalcedonies, sealing wax would not readily adhere to it. The signet or seal was important in ancient days because its imprint took the place of the person's signature. In contrast to the Egyptian custom of wearing it on a finger, it was usually suspended on a cord from the neck or arm of the Hebrew owner. Much later the signet seal was worn on a finger of the right hand by the Hebrews also.

Sardius, which is our modern sard (one of the numerous quartz varieties), was the first gemstone mentioned for adornment of Aaron's breastplate. "And thou shalt set in it settings of stones, even four rows of stones: the first row shall be a sardius, a topaz, and a carbuncle: this shall be the first row" (Exod. 28:17). (Ruby is given as an alternate in the marginal notes of the Revised Version, but commentators generally agree upon the first term.) In all likelihood the Biblical mention of this gem referred to the true red carnelian.

Josephus, writing of the breastplate gems, said, "Yet I will mention what is still more wonderful than this: For God declared before hand, by those twelve stones which the High Priest bare upon his breast and which were inserted into his breastplate, when they should be victorious in battle; for so great a splendor shown forth from them before the army began to march, that all the people were sensible of God's being present for their assistance. Whence it came to pass that those Greeks, who had a veneration for our laws, because they could not possibly contradict this, called the breastplate, The Oracle." In another allusion Josephus likened the twelve stones to the twelve months, or the signs of the zodiac of the Greeks.

One theory holds that the color of sard or carnelian is due to lengthy exposure to weather and sun. Thus ordinary chalcedony, colorless or nearly so, through the action of ultraviolet rays from sunlight, would assume a deep color from the change in the iron salts included as impurities. Greater exposure creates deeper color and greater depth of penetration; thus material on the surface is much more deeply colored than specimens dug at some depth. Yet both are undoubtedly from the same original sources. The intensely colored gems of the ancient civilizations were most likely cut out of finds from the extensive deserts of Egypt and Arabia. These were gathered as loose rocks on the surface of the sands.

In the British Museum collection of engraved gems, of 2,600 gems, 1,300 are cut from sard or carnelian, certainly evidence of the great popularity of the gem. One of the earliest Roman intaglios was discovered when Scipio Barbatus, Roman consul (298 B.C.), was disinterred during the seventeenth century. This stone, cut from sard, is part of a collection at Alnwick Castle, England. Also in an English collection is a lovely sard gem engraved to show three divisions in the life of Jonah. The stone is of exceptional luster with a reddish hue, and is believed to have been carved about the fourth century after Christ. An illustration of the seal is shown in an old book, The Life of Christ, by F. W. Farrar (former Dean of Canterbury). The fascinating volume shows many ancient engravings. Its publication date was 1874.

The name is supposed to be derived from Sardis, in Lydia, one of the numerous localities where it was obtained. It is also possible the name came from the Persian word ssered, meaning yellow. Sard, with other varieties of chalcedony, is found abundantly in the United States, in almost every state. The West Coast states have furnished some beautiful material, with Washington and Oregon having outstanding sources, as have Arizona and Colorado. Orange County and Jefferson County, New York, have sources of beautifully colored chalcedony, and many areas of Pennsylvania furnish good material.

51. SARDONYX

Sardonyx: just what the name implies—a combination of onyx and sard resembling agate in having parallel layers of two different colors, but the layers are flat rather than curved.

And the foundations of the wall of the city were garnished with all manner of precious stones. The first foundation was jasper . . . the fifth, sardonyx; the sixth, sardius. *Revelation 21:19–20, A.V.*

A cameo eleven inches wide and thirteen inches long with five layers of colors seems unbelievable. Yet one of this size, a fabulous piece, is in the Sainte-Chapelle in Paris. An even larger one, twelve by sixteen inches, is in the Vatican in Rome!

These two, presumably made of Indian sardonyx and preserved for centuries, win the unstinted admiration of modern man. They are outstanding examples of the artistry accomplished by Roman craftsmen in a period when engraved or carved sardonyxes and onyxes were extremely fine.

Early Roman writers spoke of the sardonyx as a "gem of great value" and an important material for signets. The literature of the time indicates that it was a common practice among lawyers, striving to appear prosperous and successful, to rent costly sardonyx rings to accompany an extravagant mode of living.

Sardonyx was found in India in large enough pieces to make sword hilts and dagger holds. Annual floods caused mountain streams to carry the sardonyx boulders down to the plains where men could find them. Part of the popularity of engraved sardonyxes in Rome was due to the very fine material that came in great quantity from India. By the time of Julius Caesar the desire for these gems had developed into a passion, and the Roman general was known to be an enthusiastic collector of the engraved stones.

The name "sardonyx" comes from the Greek *sardonux* and has been used for a very long time without change. Found in various areas of the East, including India, and probably Egypt, sardonyx is likely to occur in the same general areas where carnelian, onyx, sard, and other varieties of chalcedony are found. In the United States these quartz varieties are found in the Western states, Washington, Oregon, California, Idaho, and Montana all having yielded good specimens of some of the gemstones.

Some writers would identify sardius and sardonyx as one and the same, but the stones Revelation 21 lists as ornamenting the foundation walls of the New Jerusalem include sardonyx as one and sardius as another. This certainly seems to differentiate the two.

Many consider sardonyx the same as quartz onyx (two flat parallel layers), except that the white layer of agate is contrasted with a red or brown layer instead of black. Some sardonyx engravings are exquisite miniature portraits, while others depict a scene containing a number of figures. One such cameo masterpiece depicts Augustus and Roma enthroned. Before them stands a prince, and groups of captives and Roman soldiers are engraved into a lower layer of color.

The people of Pliny's time had as fine quality in the lesser gems, such as sardonyx, carnelian, lapis lazuli, and turquoise, as modern man does. Most other gems of that time were admittedly inferior to our own. At that period, however, a majority of the gemstones were found in the alluvial gravels and not dug from original sources. Pliny stated that sardonyx was imitated by a triplet of a white, a red, and a black stone, of fine quality, all cemented together.

A sardonyx was featured in a famous ring belonging to Queen Elizabeth I of Great Britain. Her portrait was engraved on the sardonyx in this ring, which she presented to the Earl of Essex as a pledge of friendship. When the earl was sentenced to death, he sent the ring by his cousin, Lady Scroop, to deliver to Queen Elizabeth. By mistake, the messenger gave it to Lady Scroop's sister, the Countess of Nottingham, an implacable enemy of the earl's who immediately realized her chance to do him harm. The countess did not deliver the ring to the queen, and the earl was executed. On her deathbed, the noblewoman is said to have confessed her crime to the queen. Elizabeth was so infuriated she shook the dying woman and cried, "God may forgive you, but I cannot!"

52. SILVER

Silver: a white metallic element, very resonant, ductile, and malleable, and capable of a high degree of polish; conducts heat or electricity better than any other known substance.

And Abraham weighed to Ephron the silver, which he had named in the audience of the sons of Heth, four hundred shekels of silver, current money with the merchant. *Genesis 23:16, A.V.*

The year 480 B.C. was a fateful one in human history.

Xerxes, king of Persia, had assembled an enormous army and fleet of ships for invading Greece. The invasion became a fact in 480 B.C., and Xerxes began to conquer Greece, for he captured Athens. Then a daring Greek naval victory changed the war's course. At Salamis the Greek fleet attacked and defeated the Persian armada. Cut off from supplies and reinforcements, Xerxes withdrew his army from Greece. Greece was saved!

Silver had paid for the fleet of Greek ships, without which Greece would surely have suffered defeat, and the silver came from the famous lead mines at Laurium. Now Greece was free to develop into her Golden Age with the beginnings of a democratic society.

An extensive mining area at Laurium, Greece, noted for its abundance of lead, produced for a millennium before the advent of Christ. The greatest activity occurred about 500 B.C. and was conducted by Athens. Though other useful minerals were found, the Athenians were principally interested in the mining of galena, a lead compound. Unusually rich in silver, it contained as much as sixty-five pounds to the ton of ore. The plentiful production of silver contributed greatly to the power and opulence of the city-state of Athens. Most of the city's distinctive coinage was minted from Laurium silver.

Silver came into use later than gold, but it was known to the Egyptians as early as 2000 B.C. as a distinct metal. Asia Minor produced silver utensils and ornaments from 3000 to 2500 B.C. Excavations of certain royal tombs have uncovered jewelry and decorations dating back to 4000 B.C. Silver was often scarcer than gold and was regarded as more valuable. In later eras, silver became far more common, and it was used as a medium of exchange, not in the form of coins but of bars which were weighed. The metal was used much like gold for decorating sanctuaries and palaces, casting idols, and making musical instruments.

The only source of silver mentioned in the Scriptures is Tarshish (Jer. 10:9). Some authorities identify this as an area of the Taurus Mountains in Asia Minor. Another reference tells of building ships at Ezion-geber, at the head of the Gulf of Aqaba, indicating that Tarshish was eastward. Now the locality is established as Spain, for the Phoenicians brought supplies of the metal into Palestine from their great colony there.

Before Israel existed, commerce had grown up between Egypt and Babylonia by trade routes across Syria. Ancient records of the fourteenth century B.C. mention silver, gold, and precious stones among articles of exchange. By the time of the Patriarchs, the use of silver and gold was current, being exchanged by weight. Joseph was sold for twenty pieces of silver, but at the height of his power in Egypt, silver failed. Then barter supplanted precious metal, and grain was purchased with cattle and land.

During the conquest of Canaan, silver money was in circulation, and gold jewelry and ornaments were used as money. Since gold was rarely used, copper some, and iron never, silver became so widely used that all money came to be called "silver." In the age of Solomon, silver was abundant, for enormous amounts were used in the Temple.

A simple ancient process for refining precious metals heated the impure mineral in a cupel, a porous cup of bone ash. A blast of air intensified the heat. Base metals, copper, iron, tin, and lead, oxidized and were absorbed in the porous cupel. The residue was a button of practically pure precious metal. Isaiah referred to this process: "And I will turn my hand upon thee, and purely purge away thy dross, and take away all thy tin" (1:25).

In New Testament accounts, silver played a significant role. Judas' greed and acceptance of the thirty pieces of silver brought the infamous betrayal of Christ.

One of the primary reasons for exploring the New World was to search for silver. Latin American mines have produced a flood of silver, and the entire Western Hemisphere has produced enormous amounts. Though usually a by-product of mining for other metals, the mineral does occur as native silver. The Anaconda Copper Company at Butte, Montana, though mining copper, secures more silver as a by-product than does any silver mine in the United States. The Bingham Canyon, Utah, copper mine ranks second in silver production. A Peruvian copper mine at Cerro de Pasco leads the world in the production of silver.

A 16,000-foot volcanic peak in Bolivia, Cerro de Potosí, is riddled with veins of silver ore. Cerro de Potosí is believed to be the world's richest mountain of silver. Discovered in 1544, it has yielded more than 2 billion ounces of the mineral.

As native silver, the mineral often forms spectacular groups of crystals. Old mines at Kongsberg, Norway, worked for several hundred years, have furnished extremely fine crystals. These mines were the source of the silver which made Sweden famous for silver-crafting. A fabulous "silver sidewalk" about 100 feet long and 60 feet thick of almost solid silver was found in the LaRose mine in the Cobalt District of Ontario, Canada.

Aspen, Colorado, silver mines frequently produce masses of matted silver wires, and in the Mollie Gibson mine at Aspen large nuggets of native silver have been found. The largest nugget weighed 1,840 pounds and was more than 90 percent silver. Discovered in 1890, it was too large to be raised in a mine bucket, so a chain was fastened about it, and it was then hauled to the surface.

Argentite, an important ore of silver, is found in Nevada at the Comstock lode, in Arizona at the Silver King mine, and on the north shore of Lake Superior at mines near Port Arthur.

Silver is more versatile in industry than gold today. Enormous amounts are used in photography. It is the most superior conductor of electricity. It is also the brightest of all metals, for it reflects back most of the light that strikes it. Silver has sterilizing properties which make it useful for purifying the water in filtering plants and swimming pools. Of course, silver is a favorite for many styles of jewelry and for beautiful and decorative objects and serving pieces in the home.

The Navajo Indians of the Southwest are superlative artists in silversmithing. Their jewelrymaking, an alien craft adopted by the Navajo, who formerly had known practically nothing of metals and their working, is the result of a Mexican silversmith who came into Navajo country about the middle of the nineteenth century. Using borrowed patterns at the beginning of their craft and adapting Mexican pesos as their source of silver, they have become world famous for their art.

53. SLIME

Slime: an archaic, Biblical term for what seems to have been a variety of pitch or possibly asphalt.

And they said one to another, Go to, let us make brick and burn them thoroughly. And they had brick for stone, and slime had they for mortar. Genesis 11:3, A.V.

Seeking absorbing, exciting adventure tales? There is no better source than the Bible. One of the most thrilling of these graphically portrays the gnawing fear troubling the Egyptian pharaoh at the multiplying number of Hebrew inhabitants and their growing power in his land. The story unfolds with the ruler's desperate efforts to suppress the Hebrews, even to murdering their newborn male infants.

Then Moses was born and successfully hidden for three months. Fearful of discovery, his Hebrew mother took a woven basket or ark, waterproofed it with slime and pitch, and placed the baby in it. Carefully she floated the container among the reeds growing on the bank of the Nile River. The discovery of the infant by the pharaoh's daughter and Moses' rise to power in the Egyptian government are familiar to everyone.

The slime and pitch daubed on the basket are ancient Biblical terms, as is bitumen, for our modern substance called asphalt. Since both "slime" and "pitch" are used in describing the waterproofing of the little basket, surely they meant different substances. They may have been differing varieties of asphalt, perhaps the same chemically (or nearly so), but of differing density. Slime could have waterproofed the surface of the ark, and pitch could have sealed the openings between the papyrus reeds. Smith-Goodspeed translates the passage: "She procured an ark of papyrus reeds for him, and daubing it with bitumen and pitch, she put the child in it" (Exod. 2:3). In all translations two substances are mentioned.

The slimepits mentioned in Genesis 14 were undoubtedly pools of asphalt soft enough to trap unwary animals and even human beings. In the first verses of the chapter, a battle of kings is described. Then: "And the vale of Siddim was full of slimepits; and the kings of Sodom and Gomorrah fled, and fell there" (Gen. 14:10, A.V.). The Revised Standard Version is even more pointed regarding the fate of the kings: "Now the Valley of Siddim was full of bitumen pits; and as the kings of Sodom and Gomorrah fled, some fell into them, and the rest fled to the mountain."

Excavations begun early in the 1900's at ancient Ur were disappointing, so a small mound, Tel el-Obeid, about four miles west of the ancient metropolis was explored. The mound revealed artifacts very different from those of Ur. A small temple, decorated with figures of lions and bulls formed of copper plates, showed that the plates were backed with slime (asphalt) to cement them to a wooden core. Tongues, teeth, and eyes of colored stones and shell were fastened in the same manner with the sticky material.

Slime, a superb adhesive, was primarily used for waterproofing. The ancient dwellers of the valley of the Euphrates achieved some spectacular accomplishments in their buildings, but they also made life easier for some of their city dwellers. The large sewers that drained the cities, even in those days of antiquity, were lined with blocks of asphalt mixed with loam and gravel. Waterproofed by the asphalt, the royal baths and drains served their purpose efficiently.

Slime was secured from natural sources, one of the likely areas being the asphalt springs on a tributary of the Euphrates that is known as the Fountains of Is.

See Asphalt; Bitumen; Pitch.

54. SOLDER

Solder: a metal, but more often an alloy of different metals, used when melted to join metallic surfaces.

> The craftsman encourages the goldsmith,
> and he who smooths with the hammer him who strikes the anvil,
> saying of the soldering, "It is good";
> and they fasten it with nails so that it cannot be moved.
> *Isaiah 41:7, R.S.V.*

The exquisite metalwork of ancient peoples is as artistic and finely done as modern pieces and can compete favorably with the best of today's work. The age of some of the pieces is almost unbelievable. Sumerian goldsmiths executed their finest work during the period about 3200–2600 B.C., five thousand years ago. The headdress of Shub-ad, queen of Sumer, found in the royal tombs excavated by Sir Leonard Woolley at Ur, is a beautiful and delicate work of art. Flowerlets of gold shower over the head from a fastening similar to a Spanish comb. Other pieces, a cape of wrought gold, heavy earrings, and numerous necklaces set with semiprecious gems, are masterpieces.

Egyptian artists, employing somewhat different styles, executed jewelry in gold almost as early as the Sumerians, creating beautiful pieces set and inlaid with precious stones. Some of these pieces date to the Age of Pyramids, about 2900–2450 B.C.

The Israelites, coming from Egypt centuries later, brought with them a background of crafts. The skilled workmen employed their art in the building of the Tabernacle. With the death of these artists, work in the crafts and other mechanical arts came to a halt, for Solomon, in building the Temple, requested that King Hiram of Tyre send him skilled workers. The artist who masterminded the intricate artwork for the Temple and its many furnishings was also named Hiram, and he was skilled in every art and craft.

Many methods of working in precious metals were evolved by these ancient artists. The metals were hammered paper thin, molded into settings for gems, worked into delicate wires, and beautifully fashioned into jewelry and ornaments. It is likely that soldering was also known, as Isaiah's reference suggests:

> The workman encouraging the goldsmith,
>   the carpenter the blacksmith,
> the solderer plating his work,
>   and fastening it tight with nails!
> (Isaiah 41:7, Moffatt)

Pliny, many centuries later, was familiar with tin-lead solder and its properties, so a low-melting alloy used for soldering gold could have been known even in the beginnings of the goldsmithing craft.

One of the many flat, oblong structures surrounding the pyramids of Giza in Egypt was a chapel chamber of an ancient tomb. The spirit of the person buried there might return to such a room to find the necessities and amusements which had occupied him while he lived. If these articles could not be supplied, paintings were substituted. Unfaded after 5,000 years of existence, murals cover the walls of the chapel chamber. One panel demonstrates the activities in a jeweler's shop. Numerous workers pursue their crafts, and some are shown hammering and soldering gold into jewelry.

To prepare a metal base for inlay work, two methods were used by the Egyptians, one of which was the building up of small fences on a metal background and soldering them into place. The use of such thin strips of metal or fine wires for building up the tiny compartments is called cloisonné work. The name of the method comes from the name for the compartments, cloisons. When the cells are filled with glass paste and fired, each little cell of brilliant color becomes enamel and the tiny fences become an integral part of the design. The second method is called champlevé. Instead of fences being soldered onto the background, the base itself is hollowed out, leaving small divisions which are also filled with paste and fired, each bright glass gem held in place by the walls of the base material of the piece of jewelry.

Etruscan artists created hollow pendants to contain a magic token. Such amulets were a necessary part of the costume. Tiny vases and small figures to serve as pendants were often created by soldering together pieces of molded gold. These metalworkers also developed to a high level the art of ornamenting a gold surface with tiny grains or globules of gold, laboriously soldered one by one to the metal base. Dots, almost indistinguishable to the naked eye, created intricate and elaborate designs achieved by the art of soldering. The frostlike appearance of such work made these ancient jewelers famous.

Much later, Roman and Greek men wore numerous, important-looking rings. The rings, while appearing extremely large and heavy, were actually hollow. This was achieved by thoroughly hammering the precious metal into thin plates and welding it, another form of soldering.

55. STIBIC-STONE

Stibic-stone: an archaic alternate name for stibnite, the mineral compound of the elements antimony and sulfur.

But when thou art spoiled what will thou do? though thou clothest thyself with scarlet, though thou deckest thyself with ornaments of gold, and paintest thy eyes with stibic-stone, thou shalt dress thyself out in vain. Jeremiah 4:30, D.V.

Jezebel! The name recalls an Oriental queen, daughter of a Phoenician ruler and consort of King Ahab of Israel. Whatever her beauty may have been, she is best remembered for her licentiousness and for turning Israel to idolatry until most of the land worshiped the Phoenician gods Baal and Astarte. Resentful of the influence of the Hebrew prophets, she vowed to destroy them and had many put to death. Her name has become a synonym for deeds that are bad or detestable. After King Ahab's death she continued her degrading influence in Israel through her son Jehoram for several years.

When Jehu, anointed king through Elisha to purge Israel, destroyed her family in battle and entered Jezreel in triumph, Jezebel determined to meet him. There, in the palace she had dominated so long, she painted her eyelids with stibic-stone, using her makeup carefully to cause her eyes to appear larger and brighter. Adorning her hair and head with the headdress of a queen (she "tired her head"), she seated herself near a latticed window to attract Jehu's attention. But that very attention which she sought resulted in her death, for Jehu ordered her thrown from the window.

St. Jerome's early translation of the Scriptures definitely names the cosmetic which Jezebel used for painting her eyes as *stibio*. The Douay Version, translated from the Latin Vulgate in the seventeenth century, carries the earlier mention of the mineral. Fourth Kings 9:30 says: "But Jezebel hearing of his coming in, painted her face with stibic-stone." *The Jerusalem Bible* (1966) uses the Hebrew term *kohl* for the mineral used for millenniums as a cosmetic. "Jehu went back to Jezreel and Jezebel heard of it. She made up her eyes with kohl and adorned her head and appeared at the window" (2 Kings 9:30).

Little jars and pots of many sizes and shapes for holding kohl and other cosmetics, and sticks for applying the kohl (burned and powdered stibic-stone), have been found in Egypt.

In addition to increasing the apparent size of the eyes, stibnite was also used for coloring the hair, eyebrows, and skin. The ancients actually named the substance from the Greek words meaning "broad" and "eye." Dioscordes reported the peculiar manner of preparing the mineral for eye coloring. Enclosed in a lump of dough, it was burned in hot coals until reduced to a cinder. Milk and wine were used to extinguish the heat, then once more the antimony was placed on coals and blown on until it glowed. Pliny said the heating was then stopped "lest it become lead." Antimony, though used by these old civilizations, was not distinguished from lead. Pliny called this mineral "stibium."

During the New Kingdom, many spoons and containers for kohl and other cosmetics were made of wood, a rare and valued material. An intriguing ointment spoon is illustrated in *The Horizon Book of Lost Worlds* by Leonard Cottrell. A water bird, skillfully carved and realistically painted, pulls a swimming girl along behind it. The bird's wings, fastened by a pin at the base of its neck, swing outward to reveal a compartment which once contained an ancient cosmetic, perhaps kohl.

The mineral compound stibnite, the stibic-stone of the ancients, is the principal source of the lustrous, silvery-white or bluish-white, brittle, metallic element called antimony. It does not tarnish when exposed to the air at ordinary temperatures, and hardens metals with which it may be combined, making modern alloys such as pewter, type metal, and Britannia metal.

The element is rarely found in pure form, and though it is widely distributed, the only important ore of antimony, stibnite, is usually found in small deposits. It is often left by circulating, hot, underground waters as replacement deposits or found in veins associated with other minerals, such as calcite, quartz, pyrite, and galena.

Stibnite often forms elongated, needle-like crystals. Though it is found in the United States, the source of the largest and finest crystals is Japan. Superb groups of crystals up to 20 inches in length have come from the antimony mines on the island of Shikoku. Antimony ore has been found in Arkansas, Utah, Idaho, Nevada, and California.

The arsenic compounds realgar and orpiment frequently contain stibnite. Since orpiment and realgar were imported by the Israelites, stibnite was probably imported with them.

The use of stibnite for darkening the appearance of the eyes survives to the present day, and is not restricted to Oriental women. Luis Marden, *National Geographic* editor, while traveling in Jordan, stopped at an isolated outpost of the Jordanian Desert Police on his way to the Gulf of Aqaba. He found the officers of the desert patrol to be handsome, virile men, whose striking appearance was accentuated by piercing dark eyes, heavily outlined in velvety black kohl. This had a very practical purpose, for it protected the eyes of the policemen from the blinding glare of the sun's rays reflected from the searing desert sands.

See Antimony.

56. SULFUR

Sulfur: a nonmetallic element occurring in nature both free and combined with other elements; occurs as yellow crystals, masses, crusts, and in powder form; is highly flammable, burning with a blue flame and releasing the noxious odor of sulfur dioxide.

Just as the sun rose over the earth and Lot entered Zoar, the Lord rained sulphur and fire from the sky on Sodom and Gomorrah, devastating those cities and all the valley, with all the inhabitants of the cities and the vegetation on the land. *Genesis 19:23–25, S.-G.*

Sulfur and molasses! What dread this folk medicine instilled in young hearts! For "thinning the blood" and miscellaneous ailments supposed to be linked to the seasons of the year, this concoction was widely used by our pioneer ancestors. But sulfur's medicinal uses go far back into history, being known as early as 3000 B.C.

Egyptian men of medicine, perhaps priests, prepared an ointment of sulfur for treating granular eyelids, recording it in the Ebers Papyrus, written about 1550 B.C. The famous library at Nineveh contained a baked clay tablet on which a simplified version of the ancient prescription was inscribed, written about 600 B.C.

When Grandmother burned a sulfur candle to "purify" the house after a bout with some contagious disease, she followed a centuries-old tradition. The Greek poet Homer's *Odyssey* relates that Ulysses called for sulfur to prevent disease after the slaying of Penelope's suitors, exclaiming, "Quickly, Dame, bring fire that I may burn sulphur, the cure of all ills."

Modern man prides himself on scientific advances and achievements, but ancient man often gained the first knowledge and made practical use of it. In the field of agriculture, fungicides, now extensively used by farmers and orchard owners, had their start in ancient Greece about 1000 B.C. One of the first references to these chemicals appeared in the writings of Homer, according to Dr. L. E. Dickens, plant pathologist at Colorado State University. Homer made specific mention of the "pest-averting" properties of sulfur.

Our complete dependence upon sulfur and its diversified uses is not much realized or appreciated by civilization today. Even man's body chemistry uses a minute amount of sulfur. His creature comforts are made possible by a lavish expenditure of that odorous mineral. From birth to death, man is surrounded by sulfur-made things, even though unaware of it. One writer has said that even in death sulfur may follow a man, for the Biblical brimstone, which is sulfur, is acknowledged as the "classic fuel of hell."

In his technical but extremely interesting book *Brimstone, the Stone that Burns*, Williams Haynes describes man's ever increasing knowledge of sulfur, its derivative, sulfuric acid, and their innumerable uses. The Romans found sulfur useful in warfare. Mixing sulfur with bitumen, tar, rosin, and other combustible materials, they made a weapon for incendiary use. The rich deposits of sulfur which supplied the material to Europe for many years were found in Sicily.

When the knowledge of gunpowder was introduced into Europe after its discovery in China about A.D. 1200, men needed still more sulfur, for 10 to 15 percent of gunpowder was sulfur. Natural Sicilian sulfur and small amounts secured from sulfur springs and volcanoes filled this additional need. In the New World, when Cortés needed sulfur to make gunpowder, a courageous officer descended into the sulfur-lined crater of Mexico's famous volcano, Popocatepetl, to secure it.

From ancient scrapings of natural deposits as a source of sulfur to securing it from deep within the earth through a hot-water process is an amazing advance, as is its constantly increasing use. But sulfur, vital as it is to modern life, apparently meant little to the Hebrews except, perhaps, in a medicinal way. Numerous hot sulfur springs dotted the landscape on both sides of the Jordan River; those in Judea have been utilized for many centuries for the treatment of rheumatic diseases and are to this day. Ruins of ancient Roman baths have been found built around some of the springs.

A strange occurrence is noted near the Dead Sea, where sulfur is found as a companion to bitumen, as in one other area, Bologna, Italy. Modern localities in the United States for sulfur include Humboldt County, Nevada, Cove Creek and Sulphurdale, Utah, Santa Barbara County, California, Cody and Thermopolis, Wyoming, and around the hot springs of Yellowstone Park, and Calcasieu Parish, Louisiana.

The final mention of the element in the Bible is found in St. John's Revelation as he describes God's wrath poured forth. "But the legacy for cowards, for those who break their word, or worship obscenities, for murderers and fornicators, and for fortune-tellers, idolaters, or any other sort of liars, is the second death in the burning lake of sulphur" (Rev. 21:8, J.B.).

See Brimstone.

57. TIN

Tin: a soft, faintly bluish-white, crystalline metallic element exceedingly rare in the native state; principal use is in plating other metals, especially iron (tinplate), as a safeguard against damaging chemical action, and as one of the major components of bronze.

This is the ordinance of the law which the Lord commanded Moses; Only the gold, and the silver, the brass, the iron, the tin, and the lead, Everything that may abide the fire, ye shall make go through the fire, and it shall be clean: nevertheless it shall be purified with the water of separation: and all that abideth not the fire ye shall make go through the water. *Numbers 31:21-23*, A.V.

It is difficult to believe that peoples of ancient cultures were acquainted with but six different metals. Yet there is a specific and definite listing of these six in the Book of Numbers. They were the only metals positively known to the civilizations existing about 1500 B.C.

The instructions which Eleazar the priest gave to Moses' warriors in the above quotation from Numbers explains that only the metals, including tin, should be counted as spoils of war taken from the Midianites. The exposure to fire—probably a method of cleansing by a brief immersion in flames to remove organic matter—would not melt either tin or lead. Following the cleansing by fire was one of water. *The Jerusalem Bible* says simply: "Whereas the gold, silver, bronze, iron, tin, and lead, everything that can withstand fire, must be passed through the fire and it will be clean, yet it must still be purified with lustral water." The lustral water involved an ancient purification rite of fire combined with water.

Goldsmiths and silversmiths of Israel recognized that tin was frequently present with the precious metals. Isaiah notes: "I will turn my hand upon thee, and purely purge away thy dross, and take away all thy tin" (1:25). Some modern translators render this as "alloy" instead of tin, and *Unger's Bible Dictionary* suggests perhaps it should have been translated "lead." Ezekiel in his parable of the dross in the furnace refers to tin as a base metal (22:18-22) compared to silver, indicating that it, with brass, iron, and lead, might be added in the process of refining precious metals.

Various sources list various dates for the beginning of the Early

Bronze Age, when the hard alloy replaced copper for implements, weapons, and many other uses. Madeleine S. and J. Lane Miller in *Harper's Bible Dictionary* suggest 3000 B.C. as an approximate beginning date for the period during which bronze was the dominant metal in Bible lands. The date, of course, differed in different cultures. Bronze was utilized in Egypt in dates placed from 4700 to 3800 B.C. by various authorities; this is believed to be the earliest use of tin alloyed with copper. Other cultures may not have used bronze for as much as another 2,000 years, though articles made of the tin-copper alloy have been found at Ur, the bronze containing 10 to 15 percent tin believed to have been made about 3500 B.C. Chariot fittings, weapons, tools of numerous kinds, and distinctive ornaments of bronze found in Persia have been dated 3000 B.C.

Demands for tin were heavy in the ancient world, predating the reference in Numbers by a long period of time. The earliest needs for the mineral must have been met by Indian sources, the material being carried westward by migrations from southern and eastern Asia toward the Mediterranean area or from nearby sources.

The source of the tin necessary for the making of bronze ceases to be a mystery about the middle of the second millennium B.C., when the Phoenicians became the masters of international trade. However, its origin prior to that time remains uncertain. Cornelius S. Hurlburt, Jr., in *Minerals and Man*, says that there is disagreement among experts as to what continent the metal may have come from, whether Europe, Asia, or Africa. Some uncertain leads point to the East as a possible source. There are well-known tin localities in Malaya, in the Indonesian islands of Sumatra, Billiton, and Bangka. One wonders if the "Indian" source of prehistoric days may have been related to these extensive occurrences of tin in a belt of placer deposits extending from Indonesia to Burma through the Malay Peninsula over a distance of 1,000 miles. However, an Egyptian source may have been much nearer to their homeland. Large tin fields have been discovered in the central part of Africa, and the usage by natives of ornaments of the metal may indicate that tin reached Egypt from this area along ancient trade routes.

In *De Re Metallica*, written by Agricola and translated by Herbert C. and Lou Henry Hoover, we are reminded of how quickly and easily sources of supplies may be forgotten. It is suggested that there may have been alluvial deposits of tin in the Mediterranean area which, once exhausted, were quickly lost from memory. Not long after 2000 B.C., most of the lands at the eastern end of the Mediterranean were using bronze.

Interested in commerce rather than conquering other lands, Phoenicia sent her sailors, the most expert navigators of the time, into the western Mediterranean and beyond. They returned with tin ore from the mouths of the Loire, the Charante, the rivers of Brittany in France, and the Scilly Islands. Their principal source of supply was the island of Cassiterides, as the British Isles were then known. The Phoenicians maintained secrecy about the location of the islands. When they built the city of Gades (the modern Cádiz) in Spain, they brought the tin from what is now the Cornwall area of modern England and used Gades as the marketplace for dispensing the valuable metal, maintaining the monopoly on it for many centuries.

Later the Romans obtained tin from the same Cornwall area, and their records are sufficiently accurate that the location of the source is certain. The tin was secured in the form of tin oxide, cassiterite (from the Greek word for tin). For a very long time the metal was found as nodules or nuggets called stream tin in placer deposits. Here it had settled, after being released from the rock in which it occurred by the long, slow disintegration process of nature. After placer deposits became scarce, "hard-rock" mining was begun for the necessary metal. The Romans are believed to have mined at what later was called the Ding Dong mine located on the Land's End peninsula. History records very little about subsequent mining at Cornwall until the twelveth century A.D. Then tin was again produced there, though it may have been from placer deposits once more. As these placer deposits were exhausted, mining in the true sense was gradually begun sometime during the seventeenth century. As machinery was developed and methods of mining improved, the deposits became so depleted that by 1960 only one important mine remained, South Crofte. In Cornwall's heyday of tin mining about two centuries ago, approximately 2,000 mines tunneled the mineral-rich rock of England's southernmost county.

During the days when the Phoenicians dominated commerce, tin was used in the manufacture of the justly famous purple dye of Tyre. Remains of ancient workshops for making this Tyrian purple have been found at Tyre and Tarentum. Here were sizable mounds of spiral shells of two types of mollusks. The ancient dyemakers extracted the juice from these mollusks by crushing the organisms in the depressions in the rocks and throwing aside the broken shells. The white liquid secreted by the mollusk changes color upon exposure to the atmosphere, becoming in succession yellow, green, and finally violet or reddish purple. The diluted juice was given a type of treatment with soda and then evaporated from tin vessels.

Since cassiterite (often called tinstone) has a nonmetallic appearance, only its heavy weight suggesting the presence of metal, it is surprising that it was discovered and used so early in ancient civilizations.

Tin does not tarnish easily and has little tensile strength or ductility, so was often made into an alloy. The metal became widely used as the chief component of pewter during the Middle Ages, being alloyed with lead, brass, or copper. Today it is principally used in making tinplate, the tin covering thin sheets of steel and comprising less than 2 percent of the total weight. This material is converted into food containers, primarily tin cans. Tubes of ointments, tin foil, and solder are also made from the metal. The tin-base material introduced in 1839 by Isaac Babbitt for making bearings made possible the development of fast machinery. Other interesting uses of tin in modern life are in the making of solder used in telecommunication, for bells and organ pipes, and in the making of bronze for architectural and sculptural uses in the arts.

Like other minerals, tin occurs in crystal form, and it has been found in fine black or brown crystals in France, England, Bolivia, and New South Wales. The United States contains no workable deposits of tin. The United Kingdom, Australia, Canada, Burma, Japan, Portugal, and Spain produce small tonnages, but 90 percent of the world's production comes from Malaysia, Indonesia, Thailand, China, Democratic Republic of Congo, Nigeria, and Bolivia. While the predominant amount of tin comes from alluvial deposits, underground mining is done in Cornwall, and in Bolivia where the deposits are located at elevations of 12,000 to 15,000 feet.

58. TOPAZ

Topaz: a mineral made up of fluorine, aluminum, oxygen, and silicon; occurs in well-formed, brilliant crystals; superior hardness makes it a highly desirable gemstone.

But where shall wisdom be found? and where is the place of understanding? . . . The topaz of Ethiopia shall not equal it, neither shall it be valued with pure gold. Job 28:12, 19, A.V.

Long ago, an illusive island called Topazios produced rare gemstones. Named for the island, they were called "topaz." To be sure, the gems were there, but if anyone except the natives wanted to find them, the island had first to be found. Usually covered by a dense blanket of fog, it lay hidden from questing mariners.

Topazios means to seek, an appropriate name, for merchant ships spent much time seeking the island. Once located, the gleaming gems were on the shore, having been readied for loading by the local inhabitants. This fanciful legend, related in *5000 Years of Gems and Jewelry*, by Frances Rogers and Alice Beard, is an ancient one.

Pliny relates that two kinds of topaz were found there. One resembled chrysoprase, with a distinctive shade of green, and yielded to the file. The other resembled chrysolite, though harder. Telling of chrysolite, Pliny accurately described true topaz! This contradiction is more puzzling than the location of the mysterious isle. At some time in history, a complete reversal in names occurred between chrysolite and topaz.

Most Bible versions give Job's description of wisdom as the "topaz of Ethiopia." Job probably meant Topazios, located toward Ethiopia from Palestine, but could have meant Egypt. Whatever the gemstone may have been, it was greatly admired, and it was called "topaz" by early peoples.

Topaz was the second stone of the first row of gems in the breastplate of the high priest (Exod. 28:17). Ezekiel, naming the precious stones covering the Prince of Tyre, names both Topaz and chrysolite (28:13, R.S.V.), and St. John, describing the foundation stones of the New Jerusalem, also mentions both topaz and chrysolite (Rev. 21:20, A.V.).

Topaz may get its name from the Greek *topazion*, and another possible source is Sanskrit *tapas*, which means fire. The gem was believed to bestow beauty, intelligence, and long life, and was symbolic of friendship. Topaz reputedly possessed strange powers; during the Middle Ages it was believed that though ruby when immersed in water would cause it to boil, topaz had the opposite effect, chilling the boiling water.

Fine topaz is not widely used in jewelry because of its cost and rarity. When it is found, it often occurs in very large crystals, so gems of considerable size may be cut from them. The stone, however, is not rated with the precious stones.

Topaz is thought of as a yellow gem and is an appropriate November birthstone, being reminiscent of autumn leaves and the glow of Indian summer. Much topaz is not yellow, but colorless or pale blue or green. Pink stones, which rarely occur in nature, are created by the careful application of slow heat to brownish topaz. The rich, imperial yellow-orange topaz of Brazil is the most prized of all colors.

Because topaz has a yellow color, other yellow-hued stones have been sold by modern jewelers as topaz, and their terms are very confusing. "Spanish topaz" is heat-treated amethyst which changes to a color much like that of true topaz. "Oriental topaz" is yellow sapphire. The stone most often confused with and sold for true topaz is citrine quartz, called "citrine topaz." Though all these gems are attractive, they do not compare to true mineral topaz, and though many stones have had the name, probably the first known gem topaz of the gemmologist was Saxon topaz or that from Brazil. John Sinkankas, gemmologist, believes topaz may have been known for thousands of years as water-worn pebbles in Ceylon gravels, but did not carry the name.

Topaz is a very complex mineral compound of aluminum, fluorine, silica, and oxygen. The fluorine makes the gem especially susceptible to etching by hydrofluoric acid in groundwaters. The prismatic crystals of topaz have a single termination, the opposite end being a flat plane where it broke from the matrix rock upon which it formed, since it has excellent basal cleavage. With a hardness of 8, topaz is a very durable stone, and it scratches quartz easily. Few gems exhibit the strange property of attracting lightweight particles of paper by static electricity. A vigorous rubbing of topaz by the fingers causes this effect.

Topaz occurs in various geological formations of rhyolite lavas, granites, schists, and similar formations. Most gem crystals, however, are found in pegmatites (coarsely crystalline dikes of granite-like composition). Topaz is often found in association with cassiterite, a tin-bearing mineral, and may be indicative of the presence of tin ore. Topaz crystals are found with tin in the Cornish mines, Saxony; Durango, Mexico; New South Wales; and Tasmania.

One of the largest uncut topaz crystals is exhibited at the American Museum of Natural History in New York. It was found in a Brazilian pegmatite, and its weight is estimated at 600 pounds. Two cut stones of amazing size are in the Smithsonian Institution's collection of gems. Of material from Brazil, one is an enormous yellow topaz of 7,725 carats. The other is blue and weighs 3,273 carats. Also in the collection is a lovely 235-carat stone from Colorado. Gemstones of topaz in the American Museum of Natural History include the colorless Maxwell Stuart topaz from Ceylon, which weighed 270 carats when cut in 1897. Another, a blue

Japanese stone called the Morgenthau topaz, is a masterpiece of gem cutting. Its 444 facets required 100 hours to cut. One of the most famous topaz gems was long thought to be a yellow diamond and even called the Braganza diamond. Found in Portugal, it weighed 1,680 carats (12 ounces) and was one of the Portuguese crown jewels.

The Ural Mountains, Czechoslovakia, Germany, and Africa have yielded good topaz. Brazil has been the principal source of production for a long time and yields several colors, including sherry yellow, pink (burnt), and pale blue; colorless crystals are also found, as well as the beautiful imperial topaz.

Fine crystals have been found in Maine, New Hampshire, and Connecticut. Utah's Thomas Mountains and California's San Diego district are famous for topaz. Colorado has several localities: Tarryall, Devil's Head, and Ruby Mountain. Extremely gemmy topaz was found on the north slope of Pikes Peak several years ago. One irregular, acid-etched piece produced 17 beautiful cut gems, the largest weighing 60.7 carats.

See Chrysolite; Quartz.

59. TURQUOISE

Turquoise: a basic phosphate of aluminum with a substantial water content; blue to green coloring, owing to a minor amount of contained copper; has long been prized as a gemstone.

The foundations of the city wall were adorned with jewels of every kind, the first of the foundation-stones being jasper, . . . the eleventh turquoise. Revelation 21:19, 20, N.E.B.

Sarabit el Khadim, in the desolate wilderness of Sinai, has a wealth of inscriptions carved by ancient miners who laboriously dug turquoise for Egypt. One foreman chiseled on a rock wall: "Behold me, how I tarried there after I left Egypt; my face sweated, my blood grew hot, I ordered the workmen working daily, and said unto them, There is turquoise still in the mine and the vein will be found in time. And it was so; the vein was found at last and the mine yielded well."

The forbidding mountains of Sinai were mining centers for Egyptian pharaohs for hundreds of years before Israel's exodus from Egypt. There they mined copper as well as turquoise. The miners went to the barren and scorched wilderness in January and fled from it in May. It has been described as possible to match in grandeur, but in grandeur coupled with desolation the area is unmatched. The wadies of Maghareh and Mukatteb still show much evidence of the age-old turquoise workings, for 39 pharaohs left their names here on inscribed records of their mining activities. The earliest goes back to Pharaoh Semerkhet (first dynasty), 3,500 years before Christ.

The New English Bible and *Good News for Modern Man* both name turquoise as a Biblical gem, though earlier translators did not. Naming the gemstones as one of the foundation stones of the New Jerusalem, both versions correspond more closely with modern findings, primarily revealed in archaeology.

Long ago Martin Luther suggested that St. Jerome's rendering of Ezekiel 1:16, using the word "beryl," would be more fittingly translated "turquoise." Certainly some disputed or obscure names for gems in the Old Testament must refer to turquoise, and it is likely that future translators will render them as the famous bluish-green gem of antiquity.

Turkistan, one of the oldest-known localities producing turquoise, may have supplied the name. The finest gem material came from several small mines in Persia. The famed Persian area of Birousa was perhaps the locality of Callais mentioned by Pliny. The Persian king was said to keep for personal use the larger and best-colored specimens from the mine. Though an ancient tradition says that Isaac, son of Abraham, was the first to open these mines, modern mineralogists feel there is no reliable record that the Persian mines, northeast of Nishabom, were worked prior to A.D. 800. Any Biblical connection with this locality would be in this case only a legendary one.

Harold Lamb, author of many acclaimed historical novels, is also famed as a student of archaeology. In his *Cyrus the Great*, an older Persian says: "And how much tribute do we pay? Now tell me, cousins, just how many wagon trains of grain, herds of cattle, how much hundred weight of dried apples and miskals of silver and turquoise?" Mr. Lamb visited the tomb of Cyrus and traveled extensively in Persia (Iran), so he knew of its turquoise production and the prevailing use of this decorative stone. Cyrus the Great, who founded the Persian kingdom in the sixth century B.C., is believed to have known and used the stone.

The oldest dated piece of jewelry is an Egyptian bracelet liberally set with turquoise. The gem material came from the ancient mining area in the Sinai Peninsula. Extensively used in jewelry of many cultures in early eras, it was prized by men as far removed as the Aztecs and the Egyptians.

Most peoples esteemed turquoise because it brought good fortune to its possessor. An Oriental proverb said, "A turquoise given by a loving hand carries with it happiness and good fortune." Belief in its good luck was current in Shakespeare's time, for he portrayed Shylock's grief over the loss of his turquoise ring. Superstitions told that turquoise grew pale when its owner sickened, losing its color entirely at his death. It would regain its lost color if placed on the finger of a new and healthy master. If poison were present, the stone supposedly sweated profusely. Turquoise was favored in Germany for engagement rings, and it was believed that if either lover proved inconstant, the stone weakened in color.

Of the microcrystalline gem turquoise and the partly microcrystalline (and partly noncrystalline) opal, the first was considered a stone bringing good fortune while the latter was formerly believed to be unlucky. Both are subject to color changes more than any other gems, which probably led to ascribing good or ill fortune to them.

Travelers visiting the Bible lands, particularly those keenly interested in the archaeology and ancient history of this area, have commented on the abundance of turquoise jewelry and adornments recovered from old tombs and ruins. Turquoise gems have usually been in greater proportion than any other precious stone. The gem, a complex phosphate of aluminum and copper, is found chiefly in arid regions, usually in sedimentary and fractured volcanic rocks. Turquoise has a hardness of from 5 to 6, and its color ranges from a delicate sky blue through various shades of green to a greenish gray.

Not only a favorite of people of antiquity and of Biblical lands, turquoise is highly valued by the American Indians, and they have created superb jewelry using it as a gem. There are numerous deposits in the United States, including some being worked centuries after having been opened by the Indians. New Mexico, Colorado, Arizona, Utah, Nevada, and California all have occurrences of the mineral, though that in the Cerrillos Hills near Santa Fe, New Mexico, is the best known.

6o. VERMILION (CINNABAR)

Vermilion: a bright, scarlet-red mineral that is a compound of the elements mercury and sulfur; had a considerable ancient usage as a pigment, providing a distinctive color.

> Woe to him who builds his house by unrighteousness. . . .
> Who says, "I will build myself a great house
>   with spacious upper rooms,"
> and cuts out windows for it,
>   paneling it with cedar,
>   and painting it with vermilion."
> *Jeremiah* 22:13–14, R.S.V.

People of our time naturally think of vermilion as the distinctive color of bright red with a prominent yellow cast. But it was not always so! In ages past, vermilion was the name for cinnabar, a red sulfide, a combination of mercury and sulfur.

Cinnabar is the only common mineral compound of mercury. It constitutes practically the only ore of economic value of this exotic element. It usually occurs in veins, often in sedimentary rocks, in both massive and earthy forms. Cinnabar is often found with iron pryrite, marcasite, and stibnite in a gangue of opal, chalcedony, quartz, calcite, and dolomite, sometimes with fluorite and barite; also with carbonaceous material in shales and slates. Although cinnabar is not often found in rocks of volcanic origin, such rocks are usually closely associated with the veins containing the mercury mineral. These igneous rocks are thought to be the original source of the metal. The mineral sometimes is found in cavities in the rock, in minute crystals of tiny six-sided prisms having pyramids on the end.

In the Mediterranean world vermilion had long been known and had been a desirable article of commerce since very early times. Practically all supplies of it were brought from Almadén, in central Spain. This mercury mine, the world's oldest, was first worked by the Carthaginians and later by the Romans, and the locality still has the most important mercury deposit in the world.

Southern Russia has furnished considerable amounts of cinnabar in recent times, while smaller quantities have come from Yugoslavia, Czechoslovakia, Bavaria, Austria, Italy, and South Africa. In the Western

Hemisphere, cinnabar has been found in various places in Mexico, Peru, and Brazil. Small quantities occur in Nevada, Utah, Oregon, Idaho, Texas, and Alaska. The most important deposits in the United States are in California, in Lake, Napa, Santa Clara, and San Benito counties. Spain, Italy, and the United States furnish about 80 percent of the world's supply of mercury. The finest cinnabar crystals ever found came from the old provinces of Kweichow and Hunan in China.

There is no doubt that vermilion (cinnabar) was principally used as a pigment, but more often in the Scriptures the name was used to represent the color rather than the mineral. The parable in Ezekiel of Ahola and Aholibah (meaning Samaria and Jerusalem) probably illustrates references to color. Ezekiel says, ". . . she saw men pourtrayed upon the wall, the images of the Chaldeans pourtrayed with vermilion, Girded with girdles upon their loins, exceeding in dyed attire upon their heads, all of them princes to look to . . ." (23:14–15, A.V.).

The use of vermilion as a pigment is illustrated in the Wisdom of Solomon, whose narrative tells of its being used to ornament an idol carved from a piece of gnarled wood. Jeremiah also tells of a similar use of the paint: "Woe unto him that buildeth his house by unrighteousness, and his chambers by wrong; that useth his neighbor's service without wages, and giveth him not for his work: That saith, I will build me a wide house and large chambers, and cutteth him out windows; and it is cieled with cedar, and painted with vermilion" (22:13–14, A.V.).

The Hebrew word *shāshar* denotes not true vermilion, the mineral cinnabar, but primarily the red ocher used in painting wood, and also the color itself. As described in the Scriptural passages quoted, the pigment was much used for the painting of frescoes, paintings made with watercolors on wet plaster. It was used, too, for drawing the figures of idols on temple walls, as well as for coloring the idols themselves. The wooden beams of houses, and often the walls, were decorated with the mineral.

The Assyrians of ancient days valued the color vermilion highly, as the sculptures of Nimroud and Khorsabad still show. The name "vermilion" is supposed to have come from India, where it was given to the red resin the natives also call "dragon's blood." Cinnabar is still used for decorating idols of some religions of that country. Another authority says the term comes from the French, meaning "little worm," because the brilliant red color of crimson was obtained from small red worms.

The native cinnabar described by the Greek writer Theophrastus is the true cinnabar, for he spoke of it as affording quicksilver, another name for mercury. The Latin name for cinnabar, *minium*, is now given to red lead, a compound of lead and oxygen. That substance was used so much in early times to adulterate vermilion that it finally got the name.

Though cinnabar continues to be a valuable source of vermilion, the commercial product of today is produced by mixing mercury, sulfur, and a solution of potash in water together in a revolving drum. The mixture, heated to a temperature of approximately 115 degrees, gradually becomes a red color. Vermilion, mercuric sulfide, is used in modern times in items from sealing wax and lipstick to rubber and paints.

61. WATER

Water: a fluid composed of two familiar gaseous elements, hydrogen and oxygen; definitely classed as a mineral.

For the land, whither thou goest in to possess it, is not as the land of Egypt, from whence ye came out, where thou sowedst seed, and wateredst it with thy foot, as a garden of herbs: But the land, whither ye go to possess it, is a land of hills and valleys, and drinketh water of the rain of heaven. *Deuteronomy* 11:10-11, A.V.

Earth, water, air, and fire—these were the four basic elements of which Greek philosophers of the fourth century B.C. believed the world was composed. Robert Boyle, chemist and physicist, destroyed this idea in the seventeenth century when he defined an element: "An element is a substance incapable of decomposition by any means by which we are at present acquainted." Water failed to meet the test as an element! Water separates easily into its components, hydrogen and oxygen.

Water has been included in the list of minerals, despite probable skepticism by some readers, because water meets the test demanded of any mineral. Like other minerals, water can be liquid, vapor, or solid, depending on conditions and temperature variations. It crystallizes beautifully in six-sided crystals of infinite variety.

Job describes the three phases of water (6:15-17; 36:27-28), as do the Psalms: "He giveth snow like wool: he scattereth the hoarfrost like ashes. He casteth forth his ice like morsels . . . he causeth his wind to blow, and the waters flow. . . . Fire, and hail: snow, vapours; stormy wind fulfilling his word" (147:16-18, 148:8, A.V.).

Palestine has but one body of fresh water, variously known as the Sea of Galilee (or Chinereth or Lake of Gennesaret or Tiberias). There is only one important river, of variable flow, with a single tributary worthy of mention. That tributary, the Yarmuk River, rises in the east in ancient Decapolis and joins the Jordan River a short distance below the Sea of Galilee.

The Jordan River begins in the north beyond Mount Hermon, flowing southward into the Waters of Merom, thence into the Sea of Galilee, 696 feet below the Mediterranean Sea. The name Jordan means "downcomer," because of the river's rapid drop. Yet in its tumbling journey down the 65-mile-long valley between the Sea of Galilee and the Dead Sea, the river loops and twists 200 miles.

Years ago Bruce Barton wrote an article contrasting the Sea of Galilee and the Dead Sea. Inspired writing, it described a beautiful body of water, laughing in the sunshine, reflecting the greenery on its banks and the overhanging trees. Men and children, birds and beasts, were attracted to the pleasant situation. Life was happy around this water—the Sea of Galilee.

In contrast was the other sea—shunned by travelers, desolate and depressing, with heavy air and bitter water unfit to drink. There were no shading trees, no nesting birds, no splashing fish. The dreary waters scarcely responded to the driving desert wind. The dismal atmosphere told of a lack of life, everything seemingly dead. It was called the Dead Sea.

Why the difference? Both seas receive the good water of the River Jordan. The Sea of Galilee gives out as much as it receives, keeping clean and fresh. The other sea is miserly, holding everything it gets, giving nothing in return. So it has become a nauseous, stagnant thing—a dead sea. One sea gives and lives. The other gives nothing and so dies!

Springs, wells, and rainfall in cisterns are the only source of domestic water. Numerous wells and springs are mentioned in Bible chronicles. Many have been lost to the memory of man through ignorance and misuse on the part of the invaders who long occupied Palestine. Since the inception of modern Israel, much study of the Old Testament regarding the location of historical water sources has been undertaken. Amazingly, clues were disclosed that led to the rediscovery of many forgotten wells. Some are again giving out life-sustaining fluid.

Dr. James B. Pritchard, leader of the University of Pennsylvania's Archaeological Expedition, became interested in Jeremiah's account of Johanan and his forces pursuing Ishmael. The story tells they "found him by the great waters that are in Gibeon" (Jer. 41:12). Tracing the reference, Pritchard and his group found the pool, only eight miles north of Jerusalem. The ancient people of Gibeon had laboriously hewn a pit 37 feet across and 82 feet deep down in the stubborn limestone. They carved a stairway into the facing of the pit and, at the bottom, tunneled 167 feet through rock, from inside the city wall to a spring outside, which acted as another access to water when the city was under siege. Here was pure water in abundance!

In 587 B.C. Nebuchadnezzar's armies overran the country. His soldiers destroyed every resource that would sustain the conquered. One of the first victims was the well at Gibeon, into which the Babylonians dumped tons of dirt and rocks, making it thoroughly blocked and useless.

Passage of time sealed it completely, erasing it from the memories of men. But the Bible has a long memory, and its story led the archaeologists to the location of the well. After being lost for twenty-five centuries, the pool of Gibeon is now cleared and flowing again.

Essentially, water was the gift of life to the people of Israel. Thus, to many, the supreme importance of Jesus' allusion to water was appreciated when he offered to them, and to all mankind, the gift of the water of everlasting life (John 4:13–14).

62. ZIRCON

Zircon: a crystal gem of the element zirconium; usually occurs in well-formed crystals with a bright adamantine luster and high refractive index; is either colorless or in hues of red, yellow, brown, blue or green.

The wall itself was built of translucent stone, while the city was of purest gold, with the brilliance of glass. The foundation stones of the wall of the city were fashioned out of every kind of precious stone. The first foundation-stone was jasper . . . the eleventh, zircon. *Revelation 21:18–19*, Phillips.

Which one of the precious gems was first known to man? There has never been a definite answer. Little is known of the zircon, for its past is hidden in long-shrouded and forgotten eras of man's history. Archaeological discoveries seem to indicate it was one of the earliest, if not the first, of gems used. Numerous carved zircons recovered from some of the oldest dated sites seem to give added proof.

J. B. Phillips, in his *New Testament in Modern English*, substitutes the name "zircon" for the unfamiliar term "jacinth" in the well-known passage in Revelation 21:19. The colored varieties of zircon have been discussed under the headings of hyacinth, jacinth, and ligure, which are archaic names for this gemstone. Under these terms, zircon is, of course, mentioned in the older Bible translations. In addition, one finds frequent descriptions in other ancient and medieval literature.

The colorless variety of zircon (produced by heating brown zircons)· might be called the poor man's diamond, as its modest cost puts it within the reach of all. Its superlative brilliance, luster, and fire have caused it to be called the "Matura diamond" (jargoon), truly rivaling the diamond in beauty.

Zircon is commonly found in the makeup of igneous rocks, and once formed, it is virtually unaffected by the processes of weathering and erosion. Its superior hardness helped it keep its original state for eons, even when geologic conditions broke down the host formation to silt, soil, and gravel. Frequently, when weathering forces and stream action wore away the original rock, virtually unaffected crystals of zircon were exposed and dropped to the ground. Here they were subjected to the forces of nature, rolling downhill or being swept downstream to become a part of a riverbank or beach. From such a source they must have originally been found by someone who realized their beauty. In the end they became a part of ancient jewelry and ornamentation.

In 1789, German mineralogist M. H. Klaproth was studying the precious stones of Ceylon. In the process he discovered the element zirconium. Because of zirconium's refractory nature, the element was not isolated in a relatively pure form until 1940. The gem zircon is a compound of the elements zirconium, silica, and oxygen, and it has the highest specific gravity (4 to 4.8) of any of the precious stones.

Zircons subjected to stream action were usually broken by pressure or by the abrasive action of the many objects with which they came in contact. Eventually these finer particles of zircon were dropped along the riverbanks and deltas, forming extensive beaches of sand which contained considerable concentrations and were rich in zircons and other heavy minerals. As the lighter mineral grains were either washed or blown away, the zircon particles and other heavy mineral grains were concentrated in greater and greater amounts.

In this manner, beaches were formed whose sands were rich enough in zircon and other heavy minerals to permit economically successful mining. On a six-mile beach near Jacksonville, Florida, the sand deposits contain about 4 percent of heavy minerals, of which nearly 40 percent is rutile and 11 percent is zircon. The recovery of these two minerals simultaneously is economically feasible, for physical separations lead to retrieval of the zircon at a purity of about 99 percent. Many similar beaches are known, including one on the eastern Australian coast near Byron Bay and one in the state of Kerala (formerly Travancore) in India on the Malabar coast.

Zirconium metal has been so difficult and expensive to extract from its ores that the process was successfully and profitably accomplished only in the past quarter-century.

The greatest consumption of the mineral element is for atomic energy purposes because of its extremely high melting point (3,380 degrees Fahrenheit) and corrosion resistance. It has many ordinary practical uses, as in the manufacture of vacuum radio and photoelectric tubes, and as an addition to the porcelain of spark plugs to curb its expansion tendencies. In medicine, its high resistance to corrosion makes it useful in screws and pins for bone repair, for instruments, suture wires, and wire gauze used in surgery. The radioactive compound zirconium 95 makes possible the observation of digestive processes by X ray. It is used similiarly in the oil industry to trace the pipeline flow of heavy petroleum products.

Despite its many beneficial uses, zirconium has a bad reputation. In its pure powdered form, it is so active toward air and water as to be a terrific hazard in handling and shipping. So, as a special safety precaution, it is usually prepared as a compound with hydrogen.

EPILOGUE

In all the discussion about the various gems and minerals mentioned in the Scriptures we can assure the reader there has been no change in the religious implication of the references quoted. Changes in phraseology often occur because of newer and different translations. And substitution of one gem or mineral name for another is frequently warranted in view of recent archaeological discoveries, when more definite knowledge is available.

There is a veritable host of legends and beliefs in the magical qualities of ancient gemstones, particularly in their ability to heal sickness or their power to protect from evil. Many are the miracles attributed to specific gems. We have mentioned but a few. A complete study would require a book.

Rarely does a new Bible translation appear which does not include references to different mineral names, naturally of interest to the Bible student, the collector, or the mineralogist. Knowing ancient history, and the revelations of archaeology, one could be certain many minerals were used in ancient times, even if not found in Scriptural accounts.

We look forward to fresh discoveries in archaeology and further translations of the Holy Scriptures in keeping with new knowledge of Biblical history, ancient languages, and cultures of great age. With this will come a new comprehension of the ancient use of other minerals and gemstones. Therefore the final and complete story has not yet been told.

R.V.W.
R.L.C.